# Spike Dykes's
## Tales from the
# Texas Tech
## Sideline

**Spike Dykes**
with
**Dave Boling**

www.SportsPublishingLLC.com

ISBN: 1-58261-265-X

Publisher: Peter L. Bannon
Senior managing editor: Susan M. Moyer
Acquisitions editor: Dean Reinke
Developmental editor: Regina D. Sabbia
Dust jacket design: Kerri Baker
Project manager: Alicia Wentworth
Imaging: Kerri Baker, Kenneth J. O'Brien, Dustin Hubbart,
    Christine Mohrbacher
Photo editor: Erin Linden-Levy
Vice president of sales and marketing: Kevin King
Media and promotions managers: Michael Hagan (regional), Randy Fouts (national), Maurey Williamson (print)

Printed in the United States

Sports Publishing L.L.C.
804 North Neil Street
Champaign, IL 61820

Phone: 1-877-424-2665
Fax: 217-363-2073
Web site: www.SportsPublishingLLC.com

This book is dedicated to my wife, Sharon, bless her heart. She stepped in as point guard on the kids' basketball teams and played first base for them when Daddy couldn't be there. All those times when you get beat and the dog won't even look at you when you come home, she was always there with support and a smile. So were my kids: Rick, Bebe and Sonny. I can't thank them enough for their patience with me. Also, if I make a nickel off this book, it will go to the Stoney Garland Fund, to help with the medical expenses for the wonderful former Red Raider who suffered a catastrophic accident in 1995. I also can't give enough thanks to all the players and coaches who made this such a fun and rewarding ride for me.

—*Spike Dykes*


This one is for K, my wife and best buddy.

—*Dave Boling*

# Contents

# Chapter 1

# Hail to the Chief

## Patting the Presidential Posterior

In the fall of 1992, my secretary interrupted a staff meeting to tell me that the president was calling. I said thanks; please tell him I'll get back to him after the meeting. She said, no, this is the president of the United States.

George H.W. Bush was going to be in Lubbock, it turned out, and he wanted to come watch us practice. That seemed like quite an honor for the Red Raiders. I had coached in Midland, where his family lived for so many years, and he apparently had been vaguely aware of me for that reason. I told him I'd be tickled to death for him to come out and see us.

There were almost as many Secret Service men as players, but he had a good time. What a gentleman; he spent a lot of time with everybody. He visited with the maintenance people and workers at the stadium, and had his picture made with anybody who wanted it. That was a great experience. He

*Spike and President George H.W. Bush (Photo courtesy of Spike Dykes)*

was clearly a guy with a passion for sports and an obvious compassion for all the people who were there working.

Beyond that, he was a person who made you feel relaxed. Maybe that's what led to my little indiscretion. Some friends like to kid me about the way President Bush's visit ended. I thanked him for coming and told him how much it meant to all of us, and that I was honored and flattered.

And as he turned to leave ... I slapped him on the butt.

It was all real spontaneous; I hadn't thought about it. He was just a good ol' boy, and I guess I wanted to make him feel at home and like a part of Red Raider Nation.

# Unpack the Boxes

As happy as I was to get to Lubbock as an assistant to Jerry Moore in 1984, and as much as I wanted to stay there for the long haul, it took us a couple years before my wife, Sharon, and I felt it was safe to unpack ... just out of habit from all the moves we'd made over the years. Even being optimistic, I figured we might be around for two or three years.

But I really had a wonderful time working for coach Jerry Moore, who was a great guy. When the head coaching job opened in 1985, I applied for the opening. I didn't think I really had a chance, but if you're a coordinator, you're supposed to do it. They hired David McWilliams, who was a good friend that I had coached against when I was at Big Spring and he was at Abilene High.

I assumed that since I had applied for the job and didn't get it, that I was going to be out looking for work. New coaches usually have a staff in mind and want to bring in their own people. I said that to David and he agreed that was often the case, but not when good friends were involved. He was very gracious and kept me on as defensive coordinator, and we had a good team that went 5-3 in the Southwest Conference ... the first winning league record in seven years.

The success of the season, in fact, earned David the job at the University of Texas. He headed off to UT after the regular season, but before we were to play Mississippi in the Independence Bowl. David kidded me that if we lost it would go on my record, and if we won, he'd get an extra "W." He was kidding, but I was so happy to have the job I'd have agreed to anything.

David made a very nice gesture when he left. We had 10 assistants and he told us that all 10 were welcome to join him in Austin. That's a rare coach who would do that. I really admired him for that. And the way it worked out was fine: Half left and half stayed.

Athletic director T Jones didn't take a lot of time offering me the job; it all happened pretty fast without any national search or trying to bring in 20 candidates for interviews. To be back in West Texas was a big deal for me. And I brought to the job a pretty simple philosophy: I was going to do the best I could with what I had; we were going to have some fun playing football; I was going to be objective and consistent with the players. And if I didn't get that done, then they didn't need to bitch about it, just fire me and get somebody else.

After we got it rolling a little bit, though, I knew I wanted to stay at Tech until I was done coaching. That's the only job I wanted. I don't want to make it sound like I turned down a bunch of offers, but I had some calls along the way. I just decided that Texas Tech was where I wanted to be; it was home, and I was going to stay there as long as they wanted me.

# Independence Day

It didn't take me long to drop below .500 as a head coach. When coach David McWilliams took the Texas job, I got promoted pretty quickly and we got busy getting ready to play a tough Mississippi team in the Independence Bowl on December 20, 1986.

What made it nice was that all the coaches were still on board except for David. Of the five coaches who were going to join him at Texas, all continued with their commitment to Tech and worked with us through the bowl game. It was a nice final roundup for the bunch, and it meant that nothing really had to change as we got ready to finish up the season. The defensive guys took care of the defense, the offensive guys took care of the offense, and as head coach, I guess I was just in charge of making sure everybody got over there for the game.

We trailed 17-7 at halftime but safety Merv Scurlark returned an interception for a touchdown and Scott Segrist kicked a field goal to tie it up for us. Ole Miss kicked a field goal early in the fourth quarter to give them the 20-17 win.

It was Tech's first bowl appearance in nine years, though, and we felt maybe we were starting to build something that had some real potential for the long run. That was a fun team that we had, loaded with overachievers. But the new head coach was off to a flying start with an 0-1 record.

I figured it could only go up from there.

## Rolling the Dice

No question, T Jones, the Texas Tech athletic director, took a chance on me. You have to remember I was a 49-year-old journeyman coach with most of my resume filled up by short stays at a ton of different high schools. They could have gone out and picked up one of those bright and shiny young coaching stars and nobody would have minded at all.

Instead, they gave me a chance, and I was very humbled by the opportunity. I will always appreciate it. They really rolled the dice and it turned into a blessing for which I will always be thankful.

Former athletic director T Jones on hiring Spike Dykes: *"I had known Spike for a long time, back when he was with Darrell Royal at Texas. I had already left that staff, but I was still close to them and I had a chance to watch him at practices. It was very evident that he was a very likeable person and a good coach.*

*"Spike is the sort of a guy who is a one of a kind. It's cliché, but what you see is what you get. He's very unassuming in terms of not seeking the limelight and the cameras; he's very quick to give the assistants and the athletes credit for what they deserve and not take it for himself.*

*"When David McWilliams went to Texas, Spike was his defensive coordinator, and it took me about an hour to make him our new head coach. There was no doubt in my mind that's what we needed. He was a product of West Texas. He grew up there; he liked Texas Tech and he wanted to stay around for a while.*

*"He also had the personality and charisma that I knew would appeal to the fans and alums there. What you have to remember is that at the time he took over, we had fan apathy and we had student apathy. Spike was very well liked across the board. He was very good internally, within the department, and was very eager to work with the alumni and at the golf tournaments and luncheons and all the PR things you have to do. He was very accessible to everybody, and the media liked to interview Spike because they never quite knew what was going to come out of him. Of course, Spike probably didn't, either.*

*"I think the players understood him as a man. He had a little bark to him now and again, but he was very softhearted personally. He could jump on them but then you'd see him with his arm around somebody walking and talking to a kid. He was a good disciplinarian who had a soft approach."*

# Spike-ism

Maybe it was a health inspector who objected out of personal hygiene concerns, but somebody asked me one time what I meant when I said about our team: "We all drink with the same dipper."

Maybe somebody thought that a program with limited resources could only afford one water bucket. It seems pretty obvious to me. It means everybody wins together and everybody loses together. We've got a set of rules and everybody follows them. Nobody's bigger than the team. And it's a message we tried to send from our first day coaching Texas Tech.

# Chapter 2

# Getting Started, 1987

## Tallahassee Bound

Athletic director T Jones and I talked about our shared belief that the best way to upgrade our program was to beef up our schedule. We needed a change in perception about our program. No question. We didn't get started by taking baby steps.

Originally, we were scheduled to open with Arkansas State. Fine. About the first of June, T came up to me and said he got us out of it.

"Good, who's going to replace them?"

"Uh, we're going to Florida State."

I told him that if we were planning on upgrading to gain more credibility, that was surely one way to do it. Those people were darned good and we had never played in an environment like that.

The Seminoles were coming off an 11-1 record, a No. 3-ranking and a Sugar Bowl win over Auburn. Meanwhile, we went into the game with what seemed like about the worst luck imaginable. In the last minute of practice on Thursday that week, we were doing some little conditioning drill and quarterback Billy Joe Tolliver sprained his ankle. It was so bad that he was on crutches Friday and there was no way in the world he was going to be able to go on Saturday.

That left us no choice but to start a transfer named Scott Toman, who had never taken a snap for Texas Tech, and who really hadn't taken very many in college football at all. All he did was play one of the most phenomenal games, given the circumstances, I'd ever seen. That was maybe the toughest defense I'd ever seen, and he just hung in there and kept making enough plays to keep us close. It was something like 20-16 heading into the fourth quarter.

They pulled away from us at the end to win 40-16, and went on to another 11-1 record and a No. 2-ranking. But for us, Scott Toman put up one of the gutsiest performances ever, and we were clearly taking our first steps on the tough road toward scheduling respectability.

Former athletic director T Jones on upgrading the Texas Tech schedule: *"The thing that we felt was so important for us to change was that we weren't getting the right kind of athletes. We needed to get better athletes and better students. Plus, we were playing the wrong teams; we didn't have a non-conference schedule that would challenge the athletes.*

*"With Spike's agreement, we both felt the athletes needed to play those great teams to get a personal idea of what it took to be in that championship class. You take your lumps for a while, but the athletes responded well. What we were trying to get through to them was that we needed to develop the mindset that we were eager to face anybody, anywhere at any time. And they sure developed that."*

# Edging the Aggies

The Texas A&M Aggies came into Lubbock as the No. 15-ranked team in the country and we managed to send them home with a 27-21 loss, mostly on the strength of two good defensive stands late in the game.

Really, that was the first big win for me as a head coach. It was important in what it seemed to say about our program and us. The Aggies had been down a bit, but they had hired Jackie Sherrill and were making great progress.

We made a statement about our readiness to play very early on as little Tyrone Thurman returned a punt 74 yards for a touchdown, and quarterback Billy Joe Tolliver hit Wayne Walker on a deep pass to give us a 14-0 lead in the game's first five minutes.

Linebacker Dwayne Jiles made a huge tackle on their fullback behind the line of scrimmage on a fourth-down attempt, and our middle linebacker Brad Hastings had about 20 tackles to lead us in a very impressive defensive effort. Boyd Cowan made the final interception to finally let us stop holding our breath.

# Nice Gesture

One of the first great surprises I had as a head coach came when we beat the Texas A&M Aggies in Lubbock my first year. Their head coach, Jackie Sherrill, had an image as sort of a tough and gruff kind of guy.

They were something like 21-point favorites and we beat them for our first win over a ranked team. A lot of coaches, caught up in the emotions of that kind of loss, can be pretty irritable afterward, or want to lash out and downplay the effort of the other team.

But Jackie Sherrill was in our locker room almost before I was. He told them how well they played and how proud he was of them. I was completely amazed. I'd never seen anything like that before. He was entirely sincere. Jackie is a good friend of mine ... especially after witnessing that thoughtful display.

# Hog Slop

You'd have to say that spirits were rising after the win over the Texas A&M Aggies, and expectations were elevated when the No. 20-ranked Arkansas Razorbacks came to Lubbock the next week.

Given those circumstances, all we did was fall on our faces, getting skunked 31-0. It's hard to play such an emotional game one week, and really play somewhat over your head to get a win, and then expect to come back the next week and be sharp. If you can do it, you're one of the top teams in the nation.

We weren't. We had a hangover from the Aggie win. I don't think fans really understand the impact of emotions in this game. I don't think you can realistically expect a team to play Notre Dame one Saturday and Decatur Baptist the next Saturday and play with the same intensity.

But that's what the good coaches manage to do and it's something I never did figure out. We had our share of great games and upsets, but we had our share of losing to teams we shouldn't have lost to.

# Spike-ism

If I had a bull's-eye on my back, it was because of not always taking care of business in the games we should have won. That's fair; I understand that. Inconsistency really hurts your fans. They get really fragile when they never know which team is going to show up. You hate it as a coach, but it's awful tough on the folks in the stands, too.

## Texas Winds

The Texas Longhorns beat us in 1987 in a wicked windstorm that came across that stadium in Austin blowing about 60 miles an hour. We played hard and pretty well in front of a big crowd, but we got down in our end in that third quarter and could not push our way out of it against the wind. They scored 24 points against us in that quarter and that was surely the difference.

A lot of coaches don't really study the forecast and prepare accordingly, but I'll tell you that we had more amateur and part-time weathermen on our staff than any other team in the country. Weather changes fast in West Texas, and when those fronts hit, it can dramatically change the way you play football.

A lot of times a game would start out calm and by the fourth quarter, the wind starts howling and if you don't have the wind at your back, you can just forget about it. One game we played in Lubbock against the Longhorns was an example. We lost the toss and I muttered to myself that we just lost the game because they'll take the wind. But they deferred the choice, so we took the wind and went up 21-0 in the first quarter.

# Smoochin' Sis

We closed down the 1987 season with one of the wildest wins you ever saw, 36-35 over Texas Christian University, and then a disappointing 10-10 tie with University of Houston.

Quarterback Billy Joe Tolliver was brilliant in the win over the Horned Frogs, who led 35-30 with two minutes left in the game. With 54 seconds left, we scored when Billy Joe threw a touchdown to Wayne Walker.

That had us rolling pretty good heading into Houston to play in the Astrodome. We were up 10-0 going into the fourth quarter but they came back to tie us. We missed a short field goal and had a lot of opportunities to win it, but we didn't play well and we didn't get it done, and we ended up 6-4-1 and not getting the bowl bid we had in mind.

# Hump Games

To have made a short field goal or to have capitalized on any of the chances we had to avoid that tie against University of Houston would have made a huge difference. A win would have meant a second straight bowl game for us, which would have been the first time Tech had accomplished that in 10 seasons. So, the Houston game was what we call a "hump" game. It would have gotten us over the hump, it would have gone a long way toward establishing us as on our way to the next level.

Over the years, we had quite a few of those, and we were in a lot of them, but we didn't win many. It's hard to do, and you don't do it by wishin', you do it by getting the job done. You remember these losses way more than anything else in your career. Coaches don't really remember the wins that much.

But in my career at Tech, we had three or four really great chances to get ourselves a win in one of these games, and we came up just short. We had a chance against Ohio State in 1990 and Penn State in 1995, and we lost them. For me, that was as frustrating as the dickens.

# Moving Violation

The first year I was head coach at Tech, we had a couple tough hombres at linebacker named Mike Kinsey and Brad Hastings. They were great players who loved contact. Maybe a little too much, in fact.

They were riding together to the stadium on Saturday morning to get taped and ready for the season-opening game when somebody bumped them at a stoplight. As the story goes, the four guys in the car that hit them got out and made some comments. Big mistake. Then things got ugly.

Kinsey and Hastings just wore them out, all four of them, right there in the intersection. This was not my idea of a sanctioned pregame warmup, but I didn't even hear about it until the middle of the next week. No charges were filed and witnesses seemed to support the players' claims that the other guys started it.

Of course, Kinsey and Hastings finished it.

# Ode to Billy Joe

In Texas we've got a classification of native sons that are known as "Bubbas." You know them when you see them. Quarterback Billy Joe Tolliver was a true Bubba. He was from a little old town and was as country as they come. He didn't try to be; he just was. His daddy ran a junkyard and Billy Joe came from what you'd call humble origins.

He was a unique character, always good with clever one-liners and always saying things that really meant a lot and had a lot more context than you could ever imagine.

Of all the guys I ever coached, I don't think anybody enjoyed playing football as much as he did. He would stay out on the field an hour after practice, throwing passes to any little kid who was out there. He simply loved playing it and being around it. And he was a great player, too, and there's no telling how many big games he had for us.

He never lacked confidence, I'll promise you that. If you took him to Mount Everest tomorrow, he would convince you he could just haul off and climb it. I wouldn't bet against him doing it, either. That's what you want in a team leader because he always, always thought he could win a game for us.

When we beat the Texas A&M Aggies in 1987, he threw a bomb to Wayne Walker late in the game and we won 27-21 at a time when they were in the top 15 in the nation. The same year we beat Texas Christian University 36-35, and with 54 seconds to go, he picked up 60 yards passing to lead us. In the Japan Bowl against Oklahoma State the next year, he played like Godzilla, passing for 446 yards.

In 1988, we were down to Texas by 17 points going into the fourth quarter, but Billy Joe just took over the game ... and this was in Austin, where that kind of thing is pretty hard to do. We got down to the end and we had a two-point con-

*Quarterback Billy Joe Tolliver (Photo courtesy of Billy Joe Tolliver)*

version attempt to win it. Billy Joe was trying to throw to Tyrone Thurman, but he was covered and he wheeled around and found Travis Price for the two points that gave us a 33-32 win.

He was just unbelievable.

Former quarterback Billy Joe Tolliver on his Tech Teammates: *"I was damn lucky to have been surrounded by some very gifted athletes who made my job feel very easy. I played with a bunch of guys who brought a ton of heart and passion to the stadium. Tyrone Thurman, Len Wright, Chris Shafer, Tommy Webb, Jessie Hurst, Charles Odiorn, Wayne Walker, Rodney Blackshear, Travis Price, Eddie Anderson, Big E Ervin Ferris, Mike McBride, Jeff Keith, Chris "Old Man" Tanner, Joe Mc Means, Phil Young, Kevin Sprinkles, and the baddest man walking the planet, Clifton Winston. These were all men of true will.*

*"The Texas Tech experience for me is summed up by simply saying, 'I would run through hell on Sunday just to do it all again.'"*

# Chapter 3

# Recruiting Red Raiders

## Selling Lubbock

Every recruit did not appreciate the joys of Lubbock and that's fine. My assistants and I didn't try to convince them that we were something we weren't. If you start trying to fool kids you'll end up with a lot of unhappy people on your team. Our town is what it is, our stadium is what it is, and the campus is what it is. If it's not for you, that's fine.

My opinion is that the key to colleges is not the buildings, not the stadium, not the trophy case … it's the people there. The people are what make you happy or sad while you're there. Yeah, you fly into Lubbock and it's not Austin. That's the way it is. But there's 30,000 students on campus and they're cute kids and enthusiastic and fun. It's not a commuter school, so most of the kids live in campus residences and that keeps everybody close. That creates a nice environment and a real "college" life to enjoy.

So, mostly what we tried to do with recruits was get them to meet as many of these good people as possible when they visited us. We encouraged parents to come to see the down-home atmosphere we had. We didn't do a lot of catered meals or anything showy, we just tried to let them know who we are and let them see that our main attitude was that we are all in it together like a family.

The other thing was that we really honestly and truly did not want anybody who didn't fit in. There were many times when we had a really hot recruit in, who would have been a great addition to our team, but we didn't try to sign him because some of our players said he wouldn't be a good fit. So, we passed on some good ones. But the positive attitude of the ones we got made it worthwhile.

## Taking Risks

I knew when I took over at Tech that my assistants and I were not going to start out getting blue-chip players right off the bat. The big recruits we did get early on were people who had one problem or another that caused the bigger programs to pass on them. There was a risk involved.

That's about what we were saddled with when we got started, and we really did stretch it thin trying to get guys. We had to take some chances and we made a few bad decisions, too. That's what happens in those situations. One thing we learned pretty quickly is that we really knew nothing about getting junior-college guys. About the time you were ready to play them, they'd be ready to leave.

Because we were taking chances on risky kids, we were about eighth in the Southwest Conference early on in graduation rates. After a couple years, we didn't have to stick our necks out so far on some guys and we moved up to second in the conference in graduation rate. I'm not sure anybody in the administration came around giving us any gold stars for the good efforts of those kids, though.

# Recruit Roulette

I've got a lot of stupid ideas, but here's my thought on recruiting: The worst place you can finish with a guy is second. If you just miss out on a kid, it means you spent a great deal of time with him and put a lot of effort into his recruitment. It also meant that you had him tentatively signed in your mind and had mentally projected him onto your roster. That leaves a big hole when he signs elsewhere. It's like getting jilted at the altar.

My assistants and I tried to be realistic; we tried to get a real early feel for what our chances were with a guy. If we had no hope, we said thanks and headed down the road. There are a million reasons why a kid might not want to go to your school. Maybe his girlfriend is going someplace else, or he doesn't want to leave home, or his mother doesn't like you.

You can't sign everybody. But you have to make damned sure that the ones you do sign can play the game. You can take a guy who may not be quite as good as somebody else and if he's willing to work, you can coach him up and develop him. But you just can't make a mistake and get a guy who won't play. You can't be getting zeros. Our coaches did a great job of identifying guys who would play for us.

## Battling the Big Boys

Sure, we fought the living room recruiting wars against Texas and Oklahoma and some of the best programs in the country. And we very seldom beat them. That's to be expected.

The first year in my tenure when we beat Texas at Austin, one of the sportswriters came in and asked me how many of our guys could have gone and played for Texas. I said I had no idea, but he could ask them if he wanted. He did. And it turned out that we had only one guy, Anthony Lynn, who was offered a visit to Texas.

That's no big deal; it just is what it is. You don't have any control over who somebody else signs. But as we went along, we upped the ante in just about every way in recruiting. We got better players, better students, better people ... and we got a lot of really good football players.

Zach Thomas wasn't recruited a bunch, surely not by Texas and Oklahoma and all of those people. And I'll tell you what: you can win games with a player like Zach Thomas.

## Recruit Rodent

Assistant coach Robert Ford and I went into a recruit's home in Houston one time and sat across from the player and his mother. As we talked, a rat crawled out from between their seats. It was below and behind them, so they couldn't see it. Which is somewhat surprising because it was the biggest rat I'd ever seen, could have whipped up on most of the cats in the neighborhood if it came down to it.

Robert almost jumped out of the room, but we had to stay cool. If we got worked up about the resident wildlife, the player and his mother would be so embarrassed that we'd never have a chance to sign him.

This dang thing just stayed there for the longest time, and we had to try to make polite conversation all the while. It finally moved on, and when we got out of that house, we both nearly fainted.

The question, of course, is whether we signed the kid. Yeah, we signed him. And thank goodness he didn't bring his pet to school with him.

# Lord Byron

Running back Byron Hanspard was a national blue-chip recruit, of course. But we got on him early and my son Rick got to know him really well. We had taken several players from his high school in Dallas, so we had some good word of mouth going for us.

Byron was very religious, and was already a lay preacher in high school. I know that schools made a big deal out of his recruiting visits. But when he came out to Tech, we didn't promise him anything. Never promised him he'd start or that we'd do anything special for him. I think that impressed him in a way. He had a very nice visit and I think he decided that Texas Tech was a place he could be comfortable.

He turned into a first-team All-American and a Doak Walker Award winner, so that speaks to his talent. It was easy to see he had every bit of that potential when we recruited him, and we knew how important he would be to our program.

*Running back Byron Hanspard (Stephen Dunn/Getty Images)*

Rick Dykes on the recruiting of Byron Hanspard: *"Two weeks before he officially committed, Byron told me that he wanted to come to Tech, but he didn't want me to tell anybody. And he meant ANYBODY. I knew he was an honest kid and trust was going to be important to him. If he felt I was going to betray his trust, I'm sure he'd have gone somewhere else. So I told no one, including my father.*

*"He was the best player I ever recruited and he was so important to us. When we got ready to go on the last visit with my father, dad said, 'What are we doing? We're wasting our time, this kid won't go with us.' Well, we got in there and he told my dad he wanted to come to Tech, and my dad responded by telling him he felt he should really keep us in consideration and not rule us out too hastily. Byron said, 'Coach, I just told you, I want to go to Tech.' Dad was so sure he was going to turn us down, he didn't even hear Byron say he wanted to come with us.*

*"When it finally sunk in, dad literally jumped and started high-fiving everybody."*

## Pedal to the Metal

I'm not proud of this, but one episode speaks to the importance of recruiting to college coaches. I was supposed to meet with running back Byron Hanspard at his home at 5 p.m. in Dallas one day. Sadly, the wife of my good friend Emory Bellard passed away and I was asked to be a pallbearer in Marble Falls that day. I surely could not refuse that duty, and I also couldn't be late for the most important recruiting visit of my career.

But I had 200 miles to travel. Well, I started going 90 miles an hour on the interstate when a guy in a sports car blows past me at well over 100. I kind of tucked in behind him, let him block for me, and I got to Dallas to meet my son Rick three minutes before we were due at Byron's house.

I was lucky, of course. And I was stupid to do it. I understand that, and thankfully nobody got hurt. But recruiting can make you stupid.

Former assistant coach Jack Tayrien on Spike's driving: *"Spike was a legend on the Texas highways. He seemingly knew every sheriff and highway patrolman. He also had every sticker from every sheriff's association stuck on the back of his big Buick. He'd spend $500 paying dues to the different associations every six months.*

*"But his claim to fame on the Texas roads was his cruise control. Some say he was the first man in Texas to have it. Little did people know, the cruise control was nothing more than a putter. Dykes would dig into his golf bag, pull out his trusty putter and jam it down on the accelerator."*

# Mea Culpa

Okay, yes, I was not always a lawful driver. I'm not proud of it. And I never had more than three or four of those policeman's association stickers on my car at one time, no matter what former assistant coaches will tell you. Those things didn't really work, anyway.

The thing about it is this: When you grow up in West Texas, you sometimes have to drive 35-40 miles to go out to eat or go to the picture show. And there's never any traffic on the highway. Traveling fast is a way of life, and you get into a habit of doing it. I'm sorry to say that I had a problem with it, and I sure did get a load of speeding tickets.

To the Texas State Patrol, I issue this apology.

# Recruit the Mothers

Mommas can make or break you on the recruiting trail. I'm not sure that winning over momma always can get you a guy, but it sure can cause you NOT to get some guy. If momma doesn't like you, you're finished. My son Rick was well liked by mothers, and I think that helped him sign Byron Hanspard and Ricky Williams.

I have to say, mommas have the best radar-detection system in the whole world. They can spot a phony the second he gets out of the car. If you go and try to sell them a bill of goods, 99 percent of the time they'll see right through it. They like to see honesty and genuine caring. That's the kind of coach they want their son playing for.

# Sell the Product

Image is image, and you have to deal with that or correct it. When I got the job at Texas Tech, we played some tough teams at times, but I felt like we didn't do a good enough job scheduling non-conference teams.

We played some patsy teams … and some of them beat us, which is a nightmare. But our goal was to win the conference or to be a factor in the race, and we knew we had to upgrade our non-conference schedule to do it.

The other benefit of that was that you could tell recruits that you're going to play Nebraska or Oklahoma or Penn State or Georgia. We tried to get the best teams we could get, and we didn't beat many of them, but we sure were able to tell recruits things like: "We're going to Tennessee next year and you'll be playing in front of 106,000 people."

Former assistant coach Doyle Parker on Spike's recruiting technique: *"I went into a home with Spike one time in Sulfur Springs trying to sign a big lineman. It was coming down between Miami and us. We were having a nice conversation and Spike saw a treadmill over in the corner of the room. He told the player's mother that he, too, had been working out on a treadmill. Did she mind if he gave this one a try? He got up there in his suit and tie, and he didn't really know how to run this thing. It started going faster and faster and beads of sweat started popping out. The recruit and I were laughing like you can't believe. Spike couldn't figure out how to slow it down or shut it off. By the time the mother got out of her chair to get that thing turned off, Spike was sopping wet with sweat and so out of breath he couldn't talk."*

## Nasty Recruiting

Everybody engages in some degree of negative recruiting whether they believe it or not. We never worried about it. If you've got 10 guys out recruiting, you can't be with all those guys all the time, and that's why you get the best assistants you can, guys you can trust, and then tell them how you want them to behave.

As much as we would like to say we never recruited negatively, I'm sure somebody said something at one time or another. But not maliciously. I know coaches say things like: "Aw, if you go to that school, they've got nine quarterbacks stacked up waiting to play."

The problems in recruiting sometimes come when you get those 90-day wonders who are trying to turn themselves into four-star generals overnight. Those guys you have to watch. But in our conference, there was a lot of stability and everybody pretty much knew each other. You knew Mack Brown at Texas was going to do it right, and R.C. Slocum at Texas A&M and Tom Osborne at Nebraska.

It was all very honorable. If you had a problem with something you heard, you'd just call these guys up and they'd look into it.

# Telling It Straight

Assistant Dick Winder was an excellent recruiter who did a great job just being himself. He wasn't one of these slick guys who can waltz into a living room. He was kind of beat up and wore out and he was really, really, really frank with kids and their families.

Because he was so honest, he grew on people and parents really liked it. They'd ask him if their son had what it took to play for Tech, and Dick would say, "Well, I just don't know … guess we'll have to see."

Players and families become attached to the coach who does the recruiting, and they all loved Dick Winder.

# A Matter of Vision

The best recruiters are about half fortune-teller. You have to be able to see into the future and project what a player can become. Assistant Dean Campbell absolutely fell in love with this kind of skinny quarterback prospect named Kliff Kingsbury.

He wasn't on any of the big recruiting lists, and wasn't really very strong and didn't have a lot of scholarships offered to him. But he was a coach's son and after visiting with him, they were convinced he could really become a great quarterback.

That skinny kid went on to lead the nation in passing.

A factor that people may not have recognized is that every coach on my staff had coached in high school. Most of our guys were lifers who may have been old and set in their ways, but they knew what a football player looked like. They knew that the important thing was to try to get a kid who wanted to come and play hard and get an education.

The staff stability we had made it easy for the coaches in the high schools we recruited to know who was going to be showing up and what they were like. Nobody on our staff was trying to move up and go someplace else, and I surely never fired a guy in all those years.

So, we had our guys spend a lot of time with the high school coaches, and spend a lot of time getting to know the recruit. We didn't recruit some of those blue-chip prospects because we didn't always agree with everybody else that they could play. Maybe that's why we didn't win a national championship.

But we always tried to be honest with them. There's things we don't have at Texas Tech, understand that up front, because we don't want somebody showing up and then bitching about it. We were going to do it all the best we could, and if we all worked together it would be a success.

Former assistant coach Doyle Parker on Spike's recruitment of Zach Thomas: *"Zach was not very highly recruited at all, and even our staff was bouncing back and forth on whether we wanted him or not. Spike went out and watched him in a playoff game, which Zach played despite having a pretty badly sprained ankle. Zach was a little small, but Spike came back convinced we had to take the kid. He said, 'This guy, playing on a bad ankle, was the leading tackler and ball carrier; this is exactly the kind of kid we want.'"*

## Spike-ism

It never bothered me one bit when a kid chose to go somewhere else. It's like a marriage. You marry the right person, it doesn't make much difference what the circumstances are. Marry the wrong one, you're not going to be happy no matter what. Same thing with recruits. You've got to marry the right ones.

# Chapter 4

# 1988

## Bad Start

We had high expectations but finished a disappointing 5-6 in 1988. Still, we were one win from going back to the Independence Bowl. It's pretty hard to open up against North Texas and lose like we did, 29-24. We started out 1-4, and fans were understandably impatient. Heck, I was, too. I think this was another one of those years when I didn't do a very good job but was lucky that we had some changes in the administration so there was nobody around to fire me.

## Desert Heat

We traveled to Tucson for our second game of the 1988 season. Let me assure you that you can still fry an egg in the end zone on September 10 in Tucson. The problem was that the locker room was like an oven; it felt like it was about 250 degrees, and it was the worst situation I'd ever seen for a visiting team. We got cooked, 35-19.

I let Arizona coach Dick Tomey hear about it, too, promising him that when they came over to Lubbock the next year, we'd have that heater cranked up nice and high. We did, too. We had an old heater in our visitors' locker room that sounded like a threshing machine, and it was going full blast. But Dick got it turned off pretty quickly.

Still, they came in with a top 20 team, and they left with a 24-14 defeat. That's turning up the heat in a different way.

## We Hook the 'Horns

We had some great wins over Texas … of course, for Tech fans, any win over Texas is a great win. But one of the most exciting was in 1988, when we scored 18 points in the final 12 1/2 minutes to win 33-32.

The Longhorns had an unbelievably powerful defensive line, so our strategy for the game was to pass against them. Of course, they knew we would try that, so their defense was stacked against the pass. But we were going nowhere when offensive coordinator Dick Winder decided to shake it up a little and run seven or eight straight times up the middle with reserve back Clifton Winston. For some reason, that just caused everything to start clicking and shift the momentum mightily.

Late in the game, receiver Eddy Anderson had to come off the field with leg cramps, but he stretched it out in a hurry and returned. Quarterback Billy Joe Tolliver called for Eddy to run a post pattern, but he adjusted his route to a flag when his defender stayed on his inside. Billy Joe read it perfectly and they connected for the touchdown.

We never saw much sense in playing for ties at Tech. So we had a two-point conversion pass called for Billy Joe to go to little Tyrone Thurman. Texas anticipated it, and had him double covered. Again, Billy Joe made a good read, ducked under a charging linebacker, and fired the ball for the game-winner to Travis Price.

Former quarterback Billy Joe Tolliver on the 1988 win over Texas: *"My best Tech memory is an easy one. Tech versus Texas, 1988, Jones Stadium. We were down in the fourth quarter due to my poor play in the third. We came storming back and erased a 17-point deficit and won it on a two-point conversion with little time left. The thing I remember the most was a fourth down and two when I hit Tyrone Thurman, who was five foot four and 126 pounds of heart.*

*"He lowered his little-bitty shoulders and Red Raidered Up on the Texas All-America middle linebacker, Britt Hager. Incredibly, that got us that extra two yards to keep the drive alive and led to our eventual game-winning score. Tyrone got hit so hard that it knocked him all the way under our bench on our sideline. That one play personifies the heart of the Red Raider player and the whole of the Red Raider Nation."*

# Little Big Man

The staff thought I was certifiably unstable when I recruited Tyrone Thurman to Texas Tech. I told head coach Jerry Moore that he was 150 pounds, but when Tyrone showed up, the coaches almost fainted.

Here are the facts: Tyrone was about five foot four and weighed 126 pounds. I had to fight pretty hard to get him on at Tech once the coaches actually saw him on the hoof. He was a little wishbone tailback who ended up being first-team All-America as a punt returner. Tacklers simply could not tackle him ... heck, they simply could not FIND him. And could he play on Astroturf. Man, he could really move on that surface.

And did he win some games for us. My Lord, he beat Texas for us in Lubbock in 1986. In the fourth quarter, he fielded a punt inside the 10, which broke a cardinal rule of ours. We sometimes didn't complain about it if the punt was a line drive and you could catch it on the fly. But Tyrone caught this one at our own four. All he did was run 96 yards for a touchdown with it.

That kid was so inspirational. I talked about him all the time after he was gone. I never let anybody think they were too small or too thin or too anything. If Tyrone Thurman, at 126 pounds, could turn into a first-team All-American, there's almost nothing that anybody can't accomplish.

One year the basketball team was low on talent and Tyrone went out and played point guard for them. I'll tell you what, nobody wanted any part of playing against him; he was a rolling ball of butcher knives.

It's also worth noting that nobody recruited him but us. Nobody wanted him. Of course, when you're five foot four, you're flying below a lot of people's radar.

## Domo Arigato ... Y'all

No question, the strangest game we ever played was against Oklahoma State in Tokyo in 1988. The place was packed and the crowd was enthusiastic, but they knew as much about football as I knew about pearl diving.

When they got in their seats, they either had black pom-poms given to them or white ones. That told them which team to root for. Now, Barry Sanders rushed for a zillion yards for OSU and quarterback Billy Joe Tolliver threw for about 500 yards, but the fans really only cheered when the teams broke from the huddle. For some reason, that little bit of choreography really tickled them.

Barry Sanders would break off a thrilling 50-yard run and they wouldn't be worked up, but, man, break that huddle, and they were really impressed.

## Billy Joe's Big Adventure

I'll admit, when we went to Tokyo to play Oklahoma State at the end of the 1988 season, we all had some troubles figuring out what time it was … heck, we weren't sure what DAY it was. That's why we ended up cutting some slack to our quarterback when he came up missing at bed check one night.

Billy Joe Tolliver was nowhere to be seen when his room was checked at curfew. We were madder than hell and I was about to suspend him … until we found him engaged in an innocent activity. In Tokyo, space is at a premium, but golf is a passion. To accommodate those two factors, they've got driving ranges built up on the roofs of some of the parking garages, and the driving ranges themselves are stacked up several levels high.

Well, it was well after midnight when somebody found Billy Joe in one of those cubicles of a nearby driving range, pounding balls out into the night sky. He wasn't out carousing with women or drinking beers; he was working on his golf game and had no concept in the world of what time it was. He apologized for missing curfew. And, hey, he was out there getting exercise.

# Chapter 5

# The Long Road

## Makin' the Big Bucks

I'd just turned 21 and was as green as a gourd when I got my first coaching job for the princely annual salary of $3,280. That was living pretty close to the bone even in 1959 in Eastland, Texas. All they asked in exchange for that big money was that I serve as assistant football coach, head basketball coach, tennis coach and golf coach. And during the school day, I taught world history, American history, Texas history and English I. There was one other course, maybe geography, but I can't recall all five of the different classes I had to try to master and prepare for every day.

My new bride, Sharon, who was my high school sweetheart, was 19 and pregnant. There were only about two places in the whole town to rent, and we didn't discover the drawback to the one we selected until the first night we moved in. It turned out that the nation's busiest railroad tracks crossed about 40 yards behind the house. Trains would rumble through there every night, but after teaching five classes and coaching four sports, getting to sleep was never a problem.

Sharon didn't complain, in fact, she couldn't have been better about being the wife of a man entering the glamorous and rewarding profession of coaching. Here's the kind of woman I married: One day when I got home, she was out on the back porch serving TV dinners to the hobos who had wandered by off the tracks.

We were so poor it's a wonder we weren't mooching food off them. But that's how she is; she's never turned down a stray cat or a hungry mouth.

# Welcome to Coaching ... You're Fired

How did I do in that first job? I got fired almost immediately. This well-traveled coaching career almost never made it out of Eastland, Texas. I started wondering if we were going to have to hop a freight with the rest of the hobos out behind the house.

It came down to a matter of principle ... and probably some Dykes stubbornness, too, to be honest about it. It started out when I felt I had to give a warning to some kids and then was forced to stand behind the punishment. School administrators apparently didn't feel as strongly about the issue as I did.

The big sin? I put a kid off the bus and made him walk home. We had just lost a basketball game and were coming home. Some of the kids were screwing around, grab-assin' and tossing around their sandwich bags.

I announced that the next guy throwing stuff was going to get put off the bus and would have to walk home. I told them to remember that we had just lost the game and they needed to settle down. It was stupid to draw a line in the sand over a little flying baloney.

Of course, about that time, a sack came flying right at me. If the kid had been as good a shot with the basketball as he was with the bag, we might have won the game. But this broke my rule, so I got the kid and put him off the bus. Come to think of it, I guess it was maybe 15 or 16 miles from the school, so, he was in for some exercise. The kid wasn't very happy, of course, and at about three in the morning my phone rang. It was the superintendent telling me I was fired. Just like that. Twenty-one years old, about to become a father, and I was fired from my first coaching job. At least we didn't have to go far if we needed to hop a freight train in the night.

My reaction might not have been very mature, given my family circumstances, but I was tickled to death to get fired. That job was so bad that getting fired felt like being paroled. Great, I thought, I can move on. The superintendent had other ideas. He said I had to finish the school year. Can you believe that? Spike, you're fired … but be at work Monday morning.

In the long run, that wasn't that bad a deal. To get fired from your first coaching job might shake you, but there's one thing you learn right off: There's a lot worse things that can happen to you. I was never afraid about keeping a job after that, or worried too much about what was going to happen with it. You come to understand that instability and change is the nature of the beast. And the sooner you learn it, the less trouble you have packing the bags later on.

# Rules of the Road

You learn a little bit after getting fired for something stupid like I did. I never had a bunch of rules. But you have to stand up for whatever it is you've put out there. You've got a few principles you've got to follow. And if you tell them something like, "The next guy to do something gets tossed off the bus," you better be ready to toss him off the bus or just be ready to shut up the rest of the season.

The problem is, anytime you lose a person, or run somebody off, everybody loses. It's a strange thing, but the few players I've run off over the years, many of them could have been the best players on the team ... no doubt. Some really good players don't feel that rules should apply to them. And you can't run a team like that.

# Spike-ism

I tell people that I was probably never really much of a coach. But the good part of it was that I didn't fool myself into thinking I was something I was not. That's where guys get into trouble. I never thought I invented football; I never thought my great expertise was going to be what made the difference. Mostly, I wanted to go have some fun and encourage the kids to have fun, too. Let's go play the game hard, and if we win, great, if we don't let's just try to get better next week.

# The Game's on Friday, Son

Although it might not work for everybody, getting fired was a positive career move for me. After finally being allowed to leave Eastland, I hooked on at Ballinger and coached for a couple years for a great guy and wonderful coach, Bob Wright.

Bob was an old-timey kind of guy who wore a fedora hat. The best lesson I learned from him came one year heading into our last and biggest game of the year, the annual rivalry game against the Winters Blizzards. This was like the Michigan-Ohio State rivalry in our part of Texas.

It turned out that the Blizzards were an aptly named opponent for the week as the weather was horrendous. Winters had a great quarterback and a really tough team, and we were going to have to be at our best to win. So we met for the first practice of the week on Monday and Coach Wright started talking to them about all kinds of stuff, like World War II heroes and being in foxholes, and didn't say a solitary word about the Winters team. You'd have no clue who we were going to play that week. Nothing.

Tuesday, a blue norther came howlin' down at us and it was absolutely frigid. The typical division of labor on our staff called for Bob to handle the offense, and they would always practice first. Sometimes when he finished with them, he'd just turn the defensive portion of the practice over to me and head down to the drugstore to drink coffee and shoot the breeze with the boosters. Well, we worked out only for about 30 minutes before Bob decided it was just too cold and headed off to parts unknown.

Wednesday was even worse, as one of the all-time, record-setting cold fronts swept over the plains. There were 50 mile-per-hour winds, with sleet blowing sideways into your face. There was no way we could practice, so we went inside for a skull session and that was all we could do. Still we had put in almost no real preparation for the big game.

I knew we were fixin' to get our tails whupped and we'd all get fired because of it. But Friday night rolled around and we played our best game of the year, winning 20-6. It was an unbelievable victory. I confessed to Bob flat out that I thought we were going to be unprepared and they were just going to grind our corn.

He said, "Son, let me tell you something about coaching kids. The No. 1 thing is getting them to play on Friday night. This was our 10th game of the year, and we'd been doing the same thing every week, and they were tired and beat up and really needed the rest more than they needed the practice."

He was absolutely right and insightful. Maybe it's something he learned down at the drugstore.

## Spike Spitz

After two years at Ballinger, coach Emory Bellard called me over to San Angelo Central High School. He was one of the great coaches; he invented the wishbone offense for Darrell Royal at Texas.

We had a nice system and a lot of good coaches, and one of the great things about the job was that I didn't have to teach so many classes. But the one I did have to teach was swimming. Oh, yeah, I'm a big swimmer. Actually, I'm more of a floater. I'm an Olympic-caliber floater. So, I made it pretty simple. I told them the secret to successful swimming was to remember to hold your breath and never get too far from the bank.

I coached there two years and was a basketball assistant, too. Really, it was one of the best jobs in the state, and it led to my first head coaching job at Coahoma. I had been a success at San Angelo, after all … nobody drowned.

# Getting Fleeced

I was about 25 when I get my first head coaching job, and it didn't really make much of a difference in my life. We had some really good kids at Coahoma and a couple great assistants.

Two of them were longtime friends, so I pooled the coaching stipends for the three of us and split it three ways. I was making a teeny bit more as the head coach, but, man, those guys worked hard and deserved everything we could get them.

We put up a 24-2 record in two years there. I think we had the best team in the state my second year, but I got so badly out-coached in the state quarterfinals it wasn't funny. Of course, the best lessons sometimes are the most painful.

White Deer High had this 300-pound coach, Collie Huffman, who really psyched me out. He got me feeling sorry for him. He used every psychological technique on me, telling how bad his poor little team was, and how they'd never have a prayer against us. I mean, this guy was a mess, an absolute mess. But he knew all the ins and outs, which refs to get, which place to play. Anything you could get fleeced on or be gullible about … man, I fell for it all.

White Deer is up on the Caprock and it's cold up there in the middle of the summer. We got up there and it was 20 degrees with a wind blowing out of the north. And the worst part about it is that when we got on the field, they outplayed us, too. We had the better team, but they just beat us.

The lesson: Never believe that crafty old son of a gun on the other sideline. And sure as heck never feel sorry for him. It took a good whuppin' to do it, but old Collie Huffman taught me something of value.

## Reality Drill

One season at Coahoma, the players were complaining about having to work too hard. We called off practice one day, put them in a bus and took them on a little field trip to reality.

We went to the children's ward at the state hospital in Big Spring. They saw what hardships were, what real challenges looked like. And let me tell you something, when we got home, they had a different perspective on a lot of things.

## Trial and Errors

Belton High offered me twice the money, so I went there for a season and was about halfway disappointed that the fans and administration were so happy with our 6-4 record. They were tickled to death. That chapped me a little because I thought we only played okay, and I started wondering about a place where they'd be that happy with that little production.

The job at Big Spring opened up the next year and it was too inviting to turn down. But I almost screwed that up, too. They had about 10 assistants there who were older guys, really proven coaches, but for some reason I felt I had to bring in my own coaches. I made it my first order of business to replace them all so I could bring in my own guys. Stupid.

It was the wrong thing to do, but I didn't yet understand that some of the very best coaches in the country—really and truly as good at what they do as Bobby Bowden or Joe Paterno—are in the junior high schools. They're there because that's what their lives are about; it's where they want to be. They're not trying to be Knute Rockne, they're just trying to do the job and help the kids for all the right reasons. These people deserve the utmost in respect. And what did I do? Run them off. Oh, man.

Really, the key to the success of most high school programs is in the junior high system. I learned that the hard way. I thought I could just round up a bunch of coaches to come in, but I ended up spending most of my time trying to rehire all the good guys I'd already fired.

# Doing It All

I swear, people see college coaches on television and in big games and think it's really something special. It is, it truly is in a lot of ways. But the real work is at the lower levels. When you coach in high schools or junior highs, you're out there mowing grass and lining the field, doing the laundry, washing the uniforms, breaking down the films, putting together your plan for the week. And then you have to get ready to teach in the classroom all day.

The big point I'm trying to make here is that I have never seen a good coach who wasn't a good teacher. I know a lot of coaches who take great pride in how well they communicate with the kids. I enjoyed teaching, although I probably wasn't as good at it as I would have liked. But that time in the classroom is very important. You can really feel the mood of the students and the spirit of the school.

## Spike-ism

If you're not careful, coaching can be all about ego. I swear there's more egotistical people in coaching than just about any profession I've ever seen.

# Big Spring, Big Hair

They called our district the little Southwest Conference because the lineup of teams—and talented coaches—made the competition so tough every week. You had to coach against the likes of Odessa Permian, San Angelo, Odessa High, Midland Lee, Midland High, Abilene High and Abilene Cooper, which went to the state finals when I was at Big Spring. Emory Bellard was at San Angelo, and there were great coaches at just about every school up and down that road.

I was really excited about coaching in that company, but, of course, the consequences are that they beat you a bunch, too. We just couldn't beat Permian, and we couldn't beat Cooper, but we beat Abilene High three years in a row, and Moby Dick was a minnow the last time that happened. We were there three years and had a 16-14 record, which was pretty good for Big Spring, and we had a lot of fun with a lot of good guys.

Three years in one spot seemed like a long time for a coach who had moved around as much as I had, so my ears perked up when the superintendent down in Alice, near Corpus Christi, gave me a call. They had a great school, and a rich football tradition but hadn't had much success the previous season.

I took the challenge, but I nearly screwed that deal up, too. For me, it was 1970 and I was young and kind of hard-headed. What I had to remember was that it was also 1970 for the players, and they wanted to have longer hair. I didn't think that was the style for a football team and I got sideways with them about it. It was a good way to lose players over something insignificant.

Hair or not, we had some good players and we made it to the state quarterfinals. The team's effort—if not their hair styles—may have caught somebody's attention, because I got a very important phone call soon after.

# Royalty Calls

University of Texas coach Darrell Royal called and asked if I wanted to come work for him in Austin. That's like God calling and asking if you want to go to Heaven. But I, of course, almost blew it. I told him that I hadn't really thought about it. He said, "Well, take your time, give it all the thought you need … I'll call you back in 30 minutes."

I had never even had a private conversation with him, but I took the job and showed up as an assistant freshman coach. Coach Royal had a nice history of giving high school coaches a chance. I stayed there five years and I learned a lot from him, but I didn't really do much to affect the course of Texas football. I had very little input on that football team. It was enjoyable, though, because of the wonderful coaches and kids.

These were the last five years of Coach Royal's career, and when he resigned, we all thought his long-time assistant Mike Campbell, a great coach, would just slide into the job. He didn't, of course, as they called in Fred Akers from Wyoming. I had expected to stay if Mike got the job, but when Fred got it, I just felt like it was time to go elsewhere. I had no problem with Fred at all, it's just that the guy that I was pulling for didn't get it and that kind of soured the deal for me.

I don't know if Fred would have wanted me to stay, so I'm not saying I turned something down, I just made it easy for him by deciding to move on.

Former Texas coach Darrell Royal on Spike: *"Spike is one of those people who was meant to coach. He was a good football man and I know he helped us a lot with our kicking game. As a head coach, he made good copy, and that was important so people would hear about Texas Tech. Obviously, with the upset wins he had there, he knew a thing or two about getting his teams ready to play. With Spike, what you see is what you get; players appreciate that, and they always had good morale."*

# New Mexico

I just wore people out calling them for jobs. Johnny Majors over at Tennessee must have gotten sick of hearing about me because I tried so hard to get on with them. I ended up getting hired as a defensive line coach at New Mexico, and was elevated to defensive coordinator the second year.

When my old friend, Emory Bellard, went over to Mississippi State, I kind of liked the idea of going with him, but it didn't turn out very well. My wife's daddy got real sick and I was stuck in Mississippi. I felt like a duck out of water and I was worried about my family, which surely made me more trouble than I was worth for Emory.

The circumstances caused me to make a rare move for a coach, stepping back from college to high schools. I got us back in Texas by taking over the program at Midland Lee High. In the last of my three years, we got all the way to the state finals and got beat by Converse Judson.

Whenever you lose a game like that, you sink lower than a whale belly, and I was pretty depressed until Christmas morning when Jerry Moore, head coach at Texas Tech, called me to join his staff.

Thank you, Santa.

# Chapter 6

# 1989

## Paying Off

The risks we had been taking by cranking up the difficulty of our schedule started really paying off in 1989. To play better non-conference opponents on the road, we felt, would condition us to the stress and challenge of taking on our conference rivals in front of their home crowds.

We had been horrible on the road; we addressed it, talked about it, worked at it, and we got better.

We opened up 3-0 that season with wins over Arizona, New Mexico and Oklahoma State before losing to a good Baylor team. A No. 19-ranked Texas A&M club came to Lubbock and we improved to 4-1 when quarterback Jamie Gill threw a clutch game-winning pass to Travis Price.

Price had suffered a sprained ankle, but still came on and made a terrific catch on a third-and-26 desperation pass with less than a minute left in the game. Jamie hit his last eight passes and the one to Travis was the best. A converted quarterback from Wink, Texas, Travis was one of the smoothest players we ever had, and one of our real quality athletes.

That was our third win over the Aggies in four seasons. What it showed was how much we had closed the talent gap in the state.

# The Road to Success

Another indicator that football fans were starting to take the Red Raiders seriously—as they well should—came on November 4, 1989. We went into Texas's Memorial Stadium in Austin and were joined by 81,000 fans, the second largest crowd to watch a football game there.

For the first time in 22 seasons, Texas Tech beat big-brother Texas in Austin. Think about that ... 22 years. That's an entire generation of Texas Tech fans who had never been able to brag to their Longhorn friends that they had won in Austin. To put that streak to an end was critically important to us.

Jamie Gill was brilliant again, and terrific when the game was on the line, just as he was that season against the Texas A&M Aggies. Jamie had been under heavy pressure the entire game, getting sacked five times. After a loss that pushed us back into a third and 26, Jamie rolled out and found our little walk-on wingback Anthony Manyweather for a 65-yard touchdown. Anthony made a nice catch over his shoulder on an out-and-up at about the Texas 30 and just blew past a couple Longhorn defenders.

Tracy Saul was brilliant for us, as usual. Although only a freshman playing free safety, he had a 64-yard punt return, and then a late interception of a Peter Gardere pass to set up

Lin Elliott's final 51-yard field goal to put the cap on a 24-17 win.

The Texas Longhorns were the third top-25 team we had beaten at that point in the season. That was a tough schedule, but we made some strides, and that day in Austin proved that we had finally learned a few things about playing to win away from home.

# Gray Day

Steve Spurrier, in his last game as head coach of Duke, brought his productive passing attack into the All-American Bowl against us on December 28, 1989. But we dominated the game and came away with a huge 49-21 win because of the unbelievable rushing of James Gray.

All he did was rush for more yards than anybody ever did in a bowl game, picking up 280 yards, four touchdowns, and the game's MVP trophy to boot. His performance allowed us to get a lead and hold onto the ball, leaving Spurrier's explosive offense without much chance to get fired up.

Gray's standout counterpart on the defense was safety Brian Dubiski, who stopped three Duke drives with a fumble recovery, an interception and a forced fumble.

It's hard to believe, but that was the first time Texas Tech had finished the season with a win since 1973. That gave us a 9-3 record and showed our fans that we were making progress. In fact, it seemed as if things were about to reach a fevered pitch. All we wanted to do was keep building and getting better.

But even at that time we could see, ominously, that we were losing a lot of talented seniors off that team.

# Modest Star

The most modest guy we ever had might have been gifted running back James Gray. He was about as sweet a guy as you could meet. Where Byron Hanspard was fast, Bam Morris was powerful, and Tyrone Thurman was quick, James Gray simply could run the football.

He wasn't fast, but he was so fluid that people just couldn't tackle him. He reminded me of Emmitt Smith. Humble, a good team player ... James Gray was one of the real fine people we had the privilege to coach.

Former assistant coach Doyle Parker on Spike's best coaching job: *"I think Coach did his best job in 1989 when we played Duke in the All-American Bowl. Probably half of our starters were walk-ons. Before the NCAA had all those rules about walk-ons, Spike used to let anybody come out who had played high school football. He actually gave them a good, honest shot, too. Consequently, a lot of kids who were overlooked got a real chance and turned into good players for us."*

# Chapter 7

# 1990

## Stuck on the Hump

The 1990 season provided the perfect example of why a coach can't allow himself to get too elated when it seems that he's got all the answers and everything's coming up aces, and he can't get too dejected when it's nothing but question marks and deuces.

Coming off a 9-3 season, the best in 12 years at Texas Tech, we felt as if we had the program steamrolling in the right direction. We had a schedule that included not only our usual challenges of Texas Longhorns and Texas A&M Aggies, but some Ohio State Buckeyes and Miami Hurricanes, as well.

Even with that murderers row of opponents, we felt that this was our "hump season." Yes, this was going to be tough. But that's what we wanted. And in that difficult schedule was an opportunity to really make some noise on a national basis.

You might have heard the noise ... it was us falling on our face. We just couldn't win for losing. We didn't have the chemistry, and crazy things happened all year. It wasn't a matter of not trying hard, and there are no big secrets to it; we just didn't do much right and we finished a very disappointing 4-7.

## Spike-ism

A lot of people want to be around when you're having the parade, but not many want to serve as pallbearer.

## Not Bad for Openers

We'd been telling our recruits that they'd have the chance to play against the showcase programs across the country. And opening the 1990 season at Ohio State seemed to qualify in that regard.

Granted, we couldn't run against that huge defense, but in front of a national audience, we were ahead 10-3 in the third quarter. Our defense forced five turnovers that game, which weren't enough to overcome our inability to punt the ball. When you play well on defense, it turns into a field-position game.

Punting becomes critical then. We had two new punters in that game, and Ohio Stadium, with nearly 90,000 Buckeye fans in attendance, was not the best place to break them in. Our starter had booted a couple that didn't work out too well. So I tried to replace him and the second guy almost kicked one into the press box. I came back to the starter and told him to go back in, and he didn't seem to want to see much more of the Buckeyes. He basically said, hey, you already fired me.

I "coaxed" him back into the game and the next one got returned for a touchdown. Punting is one of those tough deals in football. When it goes well, few people notice. When it goes bad, oh, man, you're the goat. You're either being taken for granted or you're getting criticized.

But we had our chances to make a huge statement against a great opponent in one of the best venues in college football. And we didn't get the job done.

# Air Assault

After facing the classic Big 10 bludgeoning at Ohio State, we had to take on another top 20 team—the University of Houston—which sliced us apart with a wild and prolific passing game. David Klingler just ate us alive, throwing for more than 400 yards. That didn't exactly put us in exclusive company that year, as he passed for more than 5,000 yards and 54 touchdowns.

We just tried to hang on in that game, but we got toasted 51-35 in front of our own fans. On the upside, we got a glimpse of the potential of some talented young players in quarterback Robert Hall and receiver Lloyd Hill. This was really their first exposure together and they looked darned good.

# Season Slips Away

We beat New Mexico by just two points when Robert Hall came on (after a Jamie Gill knee injury) to connect with Lloyd Hill for a late touchdown pass. That dramatic play saved us from a horrendous 0-5 start.

Baylor came to town and we welcomed them with one of our worst efforts. Our great kicker, Lin Elliott, got a field goal blocked, which almost never happened, and we just put in an awful Homecoming Game performance. Nice timing.

We once again played well against Texas A&M, ranked No. 19 at the time, but dropped a 28-24 decision. A win at College Station that year might have helped us spin that season around a bit, but their quarterback, Bucky Richardson, got off a pass under heavy pressure late in the game to keep alive the game-winning drive. If we pulled him down, we'd win. We didn't, and they won. Sometimes it's no more complex that than.

I'll never forget one aspect of that game, though. They scored shortly before halftime and they kicked off to our Rodney Blackshear. He returned it 92 yards for a touchdown. A&M was famous for its "12th-man" kickoff team, which was manned by walk-ons. Rodney ran that back for the first kickoff return touchdown against them in more than 40 years. As I understand it, that caused them to start using just one walk-on on that unit to sustain the legacy after that.

Things never got much better after that. We lost to Rice when their 70,000-seat stadium had barely 15,000 fans in it. You put 15,000 in a place that size and it looks like nothing but family members there.

*Wide receiver Rodney Blackshear (Joe Patronite/Getty Images)*

# Hurricane Hits Lubbock

What should have been an attractive ticket for our fans was the appearance of Miami in Lubbock. We can thank Notre Dame for stirring up the Hurricanes in this one. Miami was ranked No. 2 the previous week when its national championship hopes were killed by a 29-20 loss at South Bend. Hurricanes coach Dennis Erickson promised to take that loss out on the teams unlucky enough to be listed on the remainder of the schedule.

Miami's run through the last five opponents started with a 45-10 dismantling of us. We were dominated so thoroughly we finished with minus 10 rushing yards and were sacked an unbelievable 13 times. Take a moment to ponder what 13 sacks in one game can do to your offense. It may not need reiteration after that stat, but that Miami defense was swarming pack of wild dogs.

# Bad Games, Good Fans

The game against Texas the next week wasn't much better, with a 41-22 defeat. Our record was going to hell, although we managed to salvage a couple wins against Texas Christian and Southern Methodist to finish the season. We struggled in at 4-7 to badly erode the momentum picked up with our 9-3 season the previous year.

I'd like to point out, though, that the fans were remarkable that year. Nobody likes losing, of course, and ugly is ugly and sometimes there's nothing that can mask it. But those fans hung in there and the team hung in there, and that says a lot about both groups.

## Vision Quest

One of the most courageous men to play for us was safety Sammy Walker. When he was young, he lost one of his eyes in an accident. But he was one of the hardest hitters we ever had back there.

He was some kind of guy. I always thought it had to be scary to play like that because of your depth perception trying to play the ball, and the absence of peripheral vision that helps you see blockers coming up on you.

It didn't seem to bother Sammy much, though, as he was a player who played fearlessly all over the field.

# Chapter 8

# The Dykes Family

## Born to Play

Some mothers like to keep their sons away from football on the theory that they're protecting them. My momma was exactly the opposite; she wanted me to play the game before I was even born.

She was one of six girls in her family, and one of my crazy uncles kidded her when she was pregnant that she needed to be thinking of names like "Susie" or "Sally" because the little one surely was going to be another female.

My momma reared back and told him, "I'm gonna have a boy and I'm gonna name him 'Spike' and he's gonna play football." See, I had no choice … I had to play. My given name is William Taylor, but it's really been "Spike" since I was born.

# Tech Ties

I was born across the street from Texas Tech. My daddy went to Lubbock High and both of my parents attended Tech. They met there and got married.

But our home when I was born was a little tiny place called Oasis, Texas, about 78 miles west of Lubbock, where there's nothing but a cotton gin and a little store. My daddy was a cotton ginner. There were a couple of gin fires and we moved to Big Spring for a couple years and then to Corpus Christi, where daddy worked on a big refinery at the start of World War II. He finally got us back to Big Spring and then to Ballinger when he was in the dirt-contracting business ... driving a bulldozer.

I played at Ballinger High and was what I would describe humbly as a horse-dookie football player. But we went to the state finals and I got a scholarship to Rice. I was a small-town guy, only 17, when I went off to college, and I was out of place. Plus, I wasn't good enough to play there. I don't think you ever need to be pessimistic, but it's not a bad thing to be realistic, and I saw I wasn't good enough.

I just got homesick, being 400 miles away from home, so I quit when they decided they were going to red-shirt me as a sophomore. I transferred to San Angelo Junior College, you know, some place where I could get a real academic challenge.

I finished up at Stephen F. Austin, where we had some good teams and a whole heck of a lot of fun playing football. In those days they didn't let you come off the football field, so I played center on offense and linebacker on defense. How good was I? Nothing but a plugger.

Former Iowa State and Washington State coach Jim Walden on his favorite Spike story about growing up: *"Spike has one story that we make sure he told at every clinic we ever went to. The basis of the story is that he grew up way out in the middle of nowhere in West Texas and he hadn't ever been to a city. His folks hadn't been around much, either, he said. Well, they finally go into the big city and momma goes shopping, and Spike and his dad arrange to meet her at that tall hotel downtown. They sit down in the lobby and pretty soon they see these doors open up, and people get into this little room, and the doors close ... making them disappear. They hadn't ever seen an elevator. So they watched; people go in the room and, after a while, other people come out. Well, this one old gal without much in the way of looks gets in that room and about two minutes later the doors open up and the most beautiful blonde you've ever seen walks out. Spike's dad turned and said, "Son, go get your mother!"*

# Wedded Bliss

Whenever we get together, some of my coaching friends force me to tell the story of when Sharon and I were married. They seem to think it's fiction for the sake of humor ... but every bit of it is the gospel truth.

We were going to have the reception at Sharon's family's house, which was just a block away from the church. The day before the service, I was cutting some limbs out of a tree and I stuck my head into a wasps' nest. I got at least 30 wasp stings on my face. It swelled up pretty good, but the lucky thing was that I was chewing tobacco at the time, and that stuff is supposed to be a good natural medicine against stings.

So, I took that cud out and wiped it all over my face. I looked like a real handsome groom-to-be, I'll tell you.

Sharon's father then had a slight heart attack that day (some have suggested the notion of her marrying me was too much for any father to deal with, or maybe it was the look at my swollen face with tobacco juice all over it). He had to go to the hospital, but he was all right and didn't have to stay.

On the wedding day, right before the wedding march started, we heard a ruckus up in the balcony, and a big ol' dog had gotten in there. All the ushers took off trying to corner it and get it out of there. They were stumbling all over the place, turning this into a real circus.

After the dog episode, the service went well, but at the reception, one of Sharon's brides' maids fell off the porch and broke her ankle. This was getting pretty grim, so we ate our cake and headed out. The custom then was that friends would kind of chase you out of town in their cars, but on the way, one of our friends got in a rollover wreck.

A cousin, very generously, had rented the honeymoon suite for us in Big Spring, with champagne and flowers. But when we got there, the manager had given that to one of his buddies, and we got a room with no air conditioner.

The next day we headed off to Ruidoso, New Mexico, for the honeymoon. I had a '57 Chevy with six-dollar retreads all around, and three of them blew out by the time we got to the lodge where we were staying. While unloading the trunk, I dropped the keys and the trunk closed. That meant I had to take out the back seat and make Sharon crawl through that little hole with a lighted match so she could find and retrieve the keys.

Pretty soon, I ran into an old friend who asked me if I wanted to golf with him. His wife and Sharon, he said, could go for a horseback ride while we were playing. Sharon hadn't ridden before, so we should have been leery. But, hey, it was a chance to go golfing. When they were out riding, one of those mountain thunderstorms came up, and a bolt of thunder spooked her horse, which galloped in a full-speed bee-line back to the barn, scraping Sharon through the trees and bramble, leaving her with cuts and welts all over.

Finally, we went to the racetrack there in Ruidoso for a little fun. Sharon's aunt had given her two dollars to bet on the daily double. Sharon picked out two horses that had names she liked: Fancy Fool and Old Pete. These things were unbelievable long shots, like 50 or 60-to-1. I knew there was no chance, so I didn't see the point in betting on them both, but Sharon did it anyway. I, however, didn't bet with money, but I bet on one horse in the first race and then went with the favorite in the second. Of course, both of them won and I didn't have the ticket. It would have paid something like $300.

I'd call that something of a rocky start. But she stayed with me. Good gal.

# Alta Dykes

At the risk of sounding corny, I'll just come out and say it, my mother was truly the light of my life and a real inspiration to me. I must have been the luckiest guy in the whole world, I've had so many good things happen to me, but the best may have been having a mother who was so much fun, such a unique person. She was a total hoot and she loved football more than any person I ever saw.

She always told me we needed to throw the ball more. Every Sunday I heard that. She and my daughter wanted to take over the play calling for me. It was comforting to be surrounded by so much expertise.

What made my mother so special was that she just never had many bad days, and she was always there, through all those coaching moves we made. My daddy died when I was coaching in Alice just before I went to the University of Texas.

Momma was something, boy. At age 55, she decided she wanted to go to secretarial school.

In her mid-70s, she was dying of respiratory problems. I was coaching at Tech at the time, and her illness coincided with an awful five-game losing streak we had in 1993. She was in the hospital there in Lubbock, and after I left the stadium I'd go up there and spend the night with her. Forty straight nights I stayed there.

We had been losing in every way possible, and North Carolina State had just beaten us on the last play of the game in Lubbock when momma was really near the end. Here's how much she loved football. The doctor came in and she asked him how she was doing. He said it wasn't good. She said, "Well, you gotta keep me alive at least until Saturday because we're gonna beat Rice this week."

Sadly, she passed away late in the week. We went on to beat Rice and win our last five games to get a berth in the Sun Bowl. People have asked me if that was tough to deal with, but, really, it was a very special time. My daddy had died suddenly of a heart attack. That's so much different than when a loved one is sick and both of you know they're not going to get better.

That gives you a chance to really say some things that are on your mind, and do a lot of very important sharing. Strangely, in some ways, that may have been about as good a 40-day span as I've had in my life. She was in and out of course, and she was sleeping much of the time, but I got even closer to my mother during those 40 bittersweet nights at her bedside.

Daughter Bebe Petree on Alta Dykes: *"I guess I gave away all the family secrets one time when a writer from the* Dallas Morning News *came out and asked us a bunch of questions. I got in trouble. I told him that, on her deathbed, dad's mother was calling her bookie. Dad said he was afraid the NCAA was going to investigate him because of his mother.*

*"She was a real character and she loved football. She bet on games probably her whole life. She always bet on Notre Dame. I mean this, seriously, on her deathbed, she told me that she had a $100 bill in a certain book in her apartment, and she wanted me to go get it and settle up with her bookie.*

*"She was such a football fan that she told us she wanted to be cremated and have her ashes spread over Jones Stadium. Dad wouldn't do it."*

# Rough-Neckin'

Folks in West Texas are tough … and I worked with a bunch of them, especially when I hooked up summer jobs rough-neckin' in the oil fields. Folks outside of Texas may not know much about it, but that's working on the rigs drilling oil wells.

It pays a lot of money because it's such hard work, and it's so hot on those metal oil rigs. It's dangerous, too. You see a lot of the guys missing fingers and toes. But I'll tell you it's a great way to get in shape for football and it's not bad for pocketing cash in the summer.

Coaching in high schools paid so little in those early days that I'd often get back out in the oil fields during the summers to bring in some more income. It was good work.

If you can keep all your digits, that is.

# Tribe of Nomads

A coache's life can be one of shallow roots. It's toughest on the families, of course, they're the ones who really suffer. The coach is always so busy with the job that his mind is focused, whereas the family has to do most of the tough work.

Moving is always traumatic on them. A lot of places we lived, I never knew who lived next door to me because I was never home much and we weren't there long enough to build relationships. Families also are the ones who hear all the negative baloney in the stands. The coach is on the sidelines with those headphones on and he hears nothing. But the coach's wife and kids don't have headphones on, and they get an awful earful.

One time my daughter, Bebe, came home when I was in Alice and said that her friend said I had fired her father. That was tough.

I moved those kids to New Mexico when they were in high school. The real sad thing is that a coach doesn't stand much chance of being a Father of the Year candidate. When I was at New Mexico, my son, Rick, played in the state championship game, and I missed it because I was in Corpus Christi recruiting. My daughter was Homecoming queen, and I had to get my brother-in-law to escort her because I was off on a recruiting trip. That stuff hurts.

The year my son Sonny was a senior, I only got to see him play once. After the big win over the Texas A&M Aggies in 1987, we got in the car immediately and drove to Amarillo to watch him play. It was a huge win for us, and it was the only game I saw. He was a receiver ... and they won the game, too. Sonny has gone on to coach at Texas Tech, so he understands the demands the job puts on a coach.

But that's the nature of the beast. I guess that's why coaches' kids are so special. They have to put up with a lot, have a thick skin, and be real resilient. You know, they never said a word about it to me. Not one. Never a complaint, never any guilt. It's cruel but true, it's a tough situation for them. But my family was nothing but great about it every step.

Daughter Bebe Petree on Spike's postgame routine: *"He's so amazing. We had company from out of town for every game. The house was always full. After a loss, we would always take it hard and everyone in the house would be feeling down. If you lose to, say, North Texas, it really sucked badly for everybody. My dad would walk through the door and he would say, 'Somebody die? Who died? Is somebody sick? Hey, this was just a football game … we lost it and there'll be another one next Saturday.' He would then be sure to go around the room and try to cheer up everybody individually."*

## Reach Out and Touch …

I never had an unlisted phone number while I coached at Texas Tech. I didn't think that would be too much of a problem; if people had something to say, they had direct access. In 15 years I got maybe 10 harsh calls. That's not too bad.

The most interesting was one night when Sharon answered the phone. You could tell right away what was going on, and I would have hung up after a while. But she just listened and nodded her head and let this guy go on and on. After a while, she asked if he was through, then thanked him for calling and said, "We appreciate your interest in the program." She was so cool and patient with the caller.

About a year and a half later, this guy came up to her and said, "Mrs. Dykes, do you remember an obnoxious fan that called you up at home one night and gave you a hard time? Well, that was me and I've felt bad about it ever since. I drank way too much and I hurt real bad after that game."

# Chapter 9

# 1991

## Bouncing Back

Except for a season-opening win over Cal State-Fullerton, 1991 started with very little promise. We got out of the box at 1-4, with a narrow loss to Oregon at home and another on the road at Wyoming.

It took wins over the two worst teams in the Southwest Conference—Southern Methodist University and Rice—to get us back on track. Obviously, when you're finding ways to lose, it helps to face opponents who are in the same funk.

A funny thing happened in the SMU game when safety Tracy Saul made another brilliant play for us. SMU punted to Tracy, who cut toward their sidelines and raced past coach Forrest Gregg. A picture that ran in the paper the next morning showed Tracy, with the only other person in the frame being ol' Forrest, and it looked like he was fixin' to tackle him. Funny picture, although I'm sure Forrest still could have delivered a pretty good lick if he wanted to.

A fairly close, 23-15, loss at Texas didn't hurt us too badly as we finished on a roll with wins over Arkansas, No. 20-ranked Baylor and on the road in another shootout with University of Houston.

## Slippery When Wet

The Baylor game was played in a horrendous downpour, and the weatherman got a huge assist for this win. They were going in to score on us in the fourth quarter, but the wet ball popped loose and Donny Brooks picked it off and went 99 yards for the score. They didn't get seven points and we did, to make that the key play in a 31-24 win. That was one time when Lady Luck, or Dame Fortune was looking out for us. The way it seemed, though, it was about time. These things balance out, they say. And we were due.

Baylor was ranked No. 20 in the nation at the time. Artificial surfaces make games like that reasonably playable these days, but everything still gets saturated and that ball gets awfully greasy.

My theory on coaching games like that: Keep your mouth shut and go play. It seems to me that the more you talk about it, the more you draw attention to it and get players distracted by it. Shut up, buckle up, and go out and hit somebody. That's the best way to cope with it.

Still, I think that win over Baylor that year is a "W" that goes on the weatherman's record.

# Out of Bounds

Mark Bounds led the nation in punting in 1991 … and led the nation in quirky superstitions, too. He averaged 46.8 yards a punt, which was something like three yards farther than any other punter in the country. But he had 9,400 superstitions, which included wearing orange shoes with green shoelaces.

But, man, he was fearless when it came to making decisions on the field. We were playing Baylor over there in the rain, and he made a wonderful play for us. We had kind of a rule of thumb with our punter … if he saw nobody was rushing him, he could go ahead and just try to run for the first down—within reason, of course.

We had a fourth and 15 against Baylor that he decided he'd turn into a rushing attempt for himself. I about died when he took off, but he pulled it down, started running, and every Baylor player seemed to have his back turned and was entirely ignoring him. It sustained an important drive in a big game for us.

# Humble Star

Defensive back Tracy Saul was an All-American and was the only guy ever to be on an All-Southwest Conference team four years in a row, but he was the most modest guy you ever saw. He had absolutely no ego and was as outstanding a young man as I ever had anything to do with.

And could he play? Goodness. He was a two-year team captain and I know he beat Baylor two or three times just with his punt returns. One game against Baylor he had two fumble recoveries and an interception. He was just outstanding.

It's kind of funny now, after he clobbered Baylor with such regularity, that he's got a sporting goods business over in Waco these days.

# Chapter 10

# 1992

## Consistently Inconsistent

It took us until the final game of the 1992 season before we could say we'd won two games in a row. And that only brought our total to 5-6. But that didn't mean there wasn't a great deal of excitement that fall.

We got beat by Oregon on a field goal kicked on the last play of the game. And when we went to College Station to play the Aggies, they were ranked No. 5 in the country. Again, we had their quarterback almost sacked when he got loose to sustain a drive that ended in a field goal that gave them a 19-17 win.

All this drama is fine for the fans, but we were tired of being the cowboys who got gunned down in the final scene.

We finally got it straightened out and beat Texas Christian University and University of Houston in the last two games to put together our only modest win "streak" of the year.

Once again, a couple games within our grasp slipped away. It could have meant another bowl game for us. But we continued to play top-flight non-conference teams, with Oklahoma and North Carolina State both being in the top 25 when we met.

# Leaping the Frogs

If 1992 was a season of ups and downs, nothing was more symbolic of that trait than our win over Texas Christian University. We scored 24 points in the final quarter to get a 31-28 win, as we swapped four touchdowns with the Horned Frogs in the final two and a half minutes of play.

Bam Morris ran for 199 yards and quarterback Jason Clemmons forgot about his four first-half interceptions to find Lloyd Hill for a pair of late touchdowns to give us the dramatic win.

# Lloyd Hill

As a junior, Lloyd Hill was the premier receiver in the United States. He had an uncanny knack of catching anything near the sidelines. He made some of the most phenomenal catches you ever saw. He had good speed, the ability to get open, and mister when you threw the ball to the sidelines, he'd get his feet down in-bounds and he'd catch that ball.

He was the best player in the state his senior year in high school. He was from Odessa, so he was from fairly close to Tech, and he like our players and liked our program.

Sadly, he hurt his knee his senior year and he was never quite the same. It's a shame because I was certain he could have been one of the all-time great receivers in the NFL.

# Chapter 11

# Coaching Philosophies

## Simple Philosophy

Football doesn't have to be so complex. Our philosophy was a lot more streamlined than most ... okay, it was just plain simpler.

Offensively we always just tried to do what we could do best with the players that we had. If we had good rushers, we ran the ball. On defense, we always wanted to try to make the other team beat us left-handed. By that I mean that if they've got a great running back, we were always going to fully commit to stopping that guy and taking our chances with the rest of them.

In games like that, we might spend most of our preparation time over two or three days just working on how to stop their best couple plays.

It didn't always work, but we felt it was a good approach.

# Intermission

Some of the most intense coaching of the week goes on during halftimes. That's where having a veteran coaching staff is really, really valuable. It's hard to make many adjustments on the field on the fly, so you have to try to break things down and reconstruct them during that short time in the locker room.

Coaches meet as a group really quickly while players get off their feet and get re-taped if they have to. They break up with their individual groups and then we quickly meet as a team before going back out there. Fans have no idea how many games are won or lost because of what that staff of coaches is able to get done in that short time.

# Postgame Commentary

Some of the most important addresses you can give a team are AFTER games. There are two or three things that really matter in motivating a football team, in my opinion. After the game you should address what happened: Good, bad, ugly, pretty ... whatever. You need to pay homage to some. Joe, you played great; here's what you did that was so good. Everybody needs to bring that kind of effort. If you win, you say, "Let's go enjoy it and let's be proud, and then let's get ready to go play the next game."

*A calm Spike after a Texas loss (Joe Patronite/Getty Images)*

# Rockne I Ain't

I wasn't great at making speeches. You don't have to worry about motivating them much if you get kids who love to play football. Some play the game for what it can do for them, but a lot of them play because they just really love it. Those are the ones you want.

We tried not to get too heavy-handed about it, either. At a practice, if something funny happened, we'd stop and laugh at it. It's supposed to be fun. A couple times after we lost a game, instead of going through the film and picking it apart, we burned it. I'd tell them that it was too putrid to look at and nobody should ever have to look at that film again. So we'd burn it in the meeting room. They loved that. Knowing that some coach wasn't going to chew their tails over a missed block tends to really improve the disposition of many players.

After all, what happened yesterday doesn't make much difference; it's what happens now and tomorrow that are the big things. Every once in a while you've got to realize, hey, we played Texas and we didn't play very good and they just played better. Heck, the players know that, and they're more disappointed than anybody. Why get them in that room and just keep grinding their corn over it?

## Spike-ism

I worried about our consistency. One week we'd get beat by a pretty average or poor North Texas team and then the next week we'd whip up on the Texas A&M Aggies. Those things make you wonder about the job we're doing as coaches. I know fans hated this. But not more than I hated it. We would go play at Tennessee or at Penn State and play them down to the wire, or we would beat Texas A&M one week and then lose to North Texas at home.

Here's what that is: Poor coaching.

## Big Games, Small Schemes

In the 13 years I was head coach at Texas Tech, we were 6-7 against Texas and 6-7 against Texas A&M. That's not as many as you'd want to win, of course, but that seemed to me like we were catching up. In fact, we were 4-1 in our last five games against the Aggies, which made it look, to me, like we not only had caught up to them, but we also passed them. That was big stuff for us.

Those two teams could be considered our rivals, but that was a one-sided thing and we knew it. Texas looked at us like just another game, so did A&M. I know that gave us an advantage in those games.

How did we do it? Mostly, by keeping it simple. The strategy for us was always the same: Hang in there, don't try a bunch of tricks. The longer the game goes and you're still in it, the better off you are. So, we usually came into these games with a very unimaginative and low-risk offense. Simply bland and vanilla.

If you had to gamble, you did it on defense. And then you just played the heck out of the kicking game. If you do those things and then can beat them in the kicking game, you've got a great chance of winning the game.

## Old Yeller

Me, nah, I hardly ever raised my voice. Don't get me wrong, we had some yellers on our staff. You need a few to keep them on their toes and honest. But the way I felt about it is if you yell all the time, before long nobody pays attention to you. It's just not my nature. I tried to keep an even keel. I don't care how bad it got, I think I mostly saw the glass as half full. We lost some heartbreaking games we should have won, but we won some we shouldn't have, too, so it evens out in the end.

With fear of sounding like just a complete blithering idiot, I'd like to think that I was a coach who could keep the game in perspective. That's not always easy to do, either.

People have to understand that there's nobody who wants to win more than the coaches and players do.

But when you get beat, you've got to be careful that the team doesn't get so low it can't bounce back; you can't have everybody with their chins on the floor. It hurts something fierce when you put so much into a game and lose. So I always tried to find a little bit of light and say something like, "Well, we didn't do much good, but we hung in there." I always wanted to try to find something positive about it no matter how ugly it got.

Former assistant coach Jack Tayrien on Spike's relationship with players: *"They always responded to his attitude. They seemed to appreciate that he pulled no punches; he just flat out told them how it was going to be and what he wanted.*

*"They saw real quickly that he cared for them and not just winning games. There's a ton of kids who he helped just by bringing them into his office and sitting them down and telling them, just like their daddy would across the dinner table, what they had to do. There was no pretense and he didn't talk down to them. They seemed to like that."*

Former Tech great E.J. Holub on Spike: *"He's a jewel … Spike Dykes put Texas Tech on the map. He did it by bringing in good players. And with his loyalty to the school and the players, it just kept growing and growing. I know he helped us get in the Big 12 Conference and that was crucial for this school.*

*"He has a talent for knowing when to push the young men and when to give them a break. Maybe by coaching at all those little schools on the way up, where he had success all the way, he developed a knack for getting along with players and figuring out how to make them play honest and hard.*

*"That guy is a great man."*

*Former assistant coach Jack Tayrien (Photo courtesy of Jack Tayrien)*

Former assistant coach Jack Tayrien on Spike's motivational speeches: *"The biggest thing was that he could get kids ready to play. By that I mean that they would be mentally ready in terms of knowledge and preparation. So, you don't really need much beyond that. The biggest thing he reminded kids about was that they were representing their school and their families and each other. He had a great way of telling young men, without too much screaming or hollering, what it was going to take to win the game. Sure, he played up the idea that people treated Tech like the Little Sisters of the Poor. Whenever we were playing against Texas or A&M, he'd remind them that those schools didn't want them ... but we did."*

Former Tech All-American Dave Parks on Spike: *"The thing I couldn't believe, and I've never seen in another coach, is that Spike is the same all the time, winning or losing. He never panicked, never changed. Spike was Spike and nothing ever changed that. Spike is an excellent coach who lets his assistants do their jobs.*

*"I have been around that school for a long time, and I know what it was like to compete against Texas and A&M, and if we'd get one win over them every 10 years, that was about what we expected. But Spike got us to the point where we started expecting to win games against those guys.*

*"He invited me to watch practice one time and I was hooked; I started living and dying with them. I've been on the sidelines the whole time and I never once heard him jump a coach or a player. In all that time, I never saw him embarrass anybody. He'd get after a group, saying, 'Come on, we gotta get after these guys.' But he never picked somebody out or put the blame on an individual. He realized this is still a team sport. Because of that, I don't know of any player who stayed around who didn't just love him.*

*"I'll tell you, people have these roasts and make fun of guys. They asked me to roast E.J. Holub one time and I couldn't do it because you can't roast a hero. That's how I feel about Spike, too. He put Texas Tech football on the map."*

# Chapter 12

# 1993

## Downs and Ups

With the illness and passing of my mother, the 1993 season was a very emotional time for me. Again we won our opener, against Pacific, but then we lost five straight to quality teams. That included three straight road games at Nebraska, Georgia and Baylor, and then two at home against Texas A&M and N.C. State.

This was one season when our aggressive scheduling was reflected in our record. But we felt the progress of the program was more important than the record. We were about to get into the Big 12 Conference and if we were still playing a lot of Fullertons and Arkansas States, we might not be invited in. Plus, the fan interest would be lessened, and there's also less chance of getting television exposure.

I will be honest and tell you that after five straight losses, the natives were getting a little restless. We had won nine games in 1989, and here we were unable to beat Molly

*Defensive back Marcus Coleman (Al Bello/Getty Images)*

Brown. I understand the pressure. If you're coaching and fans are booing, you're still a lot better off than a lot of folks. Even when things are bad, you have to remember that it's only a game and it's only a job. I never once felt sorry for myself as a coach. The ball takes funny bounces and sometimes you win and sometimes you don't. It's as simple as that.

But while we took our whippins early in the year, we bounced back strong with five straight wins, including another big win at Austin against Texas. Winds were blowing over 30 miles an hour and the wind chill at kickoff was 18 degrees. Games in those conditions usually turn into defensive battles. And we just played great defense in that one with four turnovers leading to 17 points in a 31-22 win.

Bam Morris had another big day with 169 rushing yards, but Marcus Coleman, who picked off a pass and ran 54 yards with it for our final score, made the final critical play.

# Oklahoma!

We'd gone three seasons without a bowl appearance, so getting back to the postseason felt pretty darned good for us. And the Sun Bowl was a nice honor for us. But Oklahoma had a great defensive team and we took a beating to the tune of 41-10. We weren't as good as they were, and we just sorta stunk it up.

Robert Hall had a wonderful season, but the Oklahoma defense picked him off four times to leave us without much offense. On the defensive side, though, linebacker Zach Thomas set an NCAA bowl record with seven tackles for losses. Nice job, Zach. That's continuing to play inspired ball even in a game that was out of reach.

# Surprise Walk-on

Robert Hall passed for 48 touchdowns and almost 8,000 yards at Texas Tech ... not bad for a guy who didn't have a scholarship when he showed up in Lubbock.

He was from Dallas Carter High School, and we liked him and recruited him, but we had too many quarterback commitments early and it left us with nothing for him. Thank goodness he came anyway.

Robert was kinda little and sorta slight, but all he did was win and win and win. He was quite a guy, a real quiet leader who led by example. He was so quiet you wouldn't even know he was there, except he was such a tremendous athlete and a tremendous person with a great feel for how to play the game.

# Worst Losses

Hands down, our Cotton Bowl loss in 1994 will never go away; I was never more embarrassed on the sidelines. We actually played pretty well; it was just that Southern California was just so much better than we were.

One that liked to kill us was the North Carolina State game in 1993 when all we had to do was make one first down to run the clock out on a win. Bam Morris, our All-American who led the nation in scoring, got the first down, but lost a fumble. They went 80 yards in 40 seconds to beat us 36-34.

We got ourselves in that famous "prevent" defense. All those people who love to criticize this defensive tactic saw exactly the reason for their feelings. Nobody mentions it if you win, of course, but when you get burned with it, you hear plenty about it.

Georgia did that to us once, too, when they went something like 80 yards in 20 seconds. That was mostly a case of the Bulldogs just executing a pass play perfectly.

Those kinds of losses absolutely rip your heart out.

# Chapter 13

# Quotes and Quips

## Figures of Speech

Some members of the media may not have always appreciated my efforts, but others tended to be amused by the little bits of West Texas commentary that slipped out every now and again. I think I've carried those things around with me since I was five or six years old sitting around my daddy's cotton gin.

Those cotton farmers would bring in their crops to be ginned, and they'd have to wait around until it was ready. Some of them went back to the farm, but a lot of them stayed there, sat around a pot-bellied stove and visited. There was always a dominoes table and a bottle of whiskey handy, and, man, they used them both. I was just a little kid hanging around there when they'd start telling stories and getting each other laughing. It was a magical time for a kid, and some of those stories have stayed with me all those years.

To me, my mother's daddy, Horace Taylor, was a great philosopher, a real colorful character, and unbelievably funny. He was an influence. And working out in the oil fields with those ol' boys was another place I was exposed to some real genuine characters.

You can't prepare those comments; they just jump out on their own. But I believe that you can sometimes say something with one quick adage that gets the message across and tells the story better than a bunch of long words. That's one thing about those people; they don't tend to have communication problems. They tell you what they're thinking.

## Press Box Crew

I never saw the media as my adversary. Of course, the media/coach relationship has changed over the years. Especially early on, I loved the media. I have nothing but bouquets for the media. The beat writers we had when we started were great guys.

All the while, we had guys who followed us, and we allowed them free access to anything they wanted to do, and for the most part, the media was very good to us.

Sensationalism and negativism are more prevalent than they used to be. As it wore on, we got newer and younger guys, and the tone changed. Then the talk-radio shows came in, and that changed everything. Nothing with them has to be founded in fact, and nobody is held accountable. A guy can call in and say he saw four players drunk in some bar, even if he's just making it up or he's got some ax to grind. They can say anything, and for a college football program, I don't think it's a good thing.

I will say that the media has always been fair to me. That's not to say they always loved me. We had a couple in Lubbock, who, I guarantee you, had a victory dance when I left. I had been there a long time. I was head coach for 13 years, and some of them were probably tired of me.

Coaches need to realize how important a relationship with the media is to the program. The thing is, though, I'd love to see more members of the media take more time going with you to the children's hospitals when the players are in there, and see some of the great things they do in the community. The media isn't always around for those kinds of stories.

Former Iowa State and Washington State coach Jim Walden on Spike: *"That man just has a great outlook on life … and funny, aw man, let me tell you. I put together a golf outing of coaches and their wives at a resort in Coeur d'Alene, Idaho. After golfing one day, we were sitting around a bar in the hotel overlooking Lake Coeur d'Alene.*

*"They had one of those boats pulling around people hanging from parachutes. We had been having a few cocktails and joking around, and we all decided that this parasailing was not really something any of us would want to try.*

*"We were gabbing and joking and having fun, and we looked up, and here comes this guy flying in that parachute wearing blue jeans and cowboy boots. No swimsuit, just full cowboy regalia. My God, it was Spike. As he flew past, he was waving and grinning at us. We were on the floor laughing so hard we couldn't get our breath … we almost died from laughing so hard.*

*"Well, Spike came back and just grinned and said, 'What do you think about that, boys?'*

*"Funniest thing I've ever seen in my life."*

Former quarterback Billy Joe Tolliver on Spike's verbal (and wrestling) talents: *"Coach and I didn't joke around too much. He was always busy trying to figure out how to stop our opponent from scoring. He placed all his trust in Dick Winder to run our offense, so he didn't say much to me during the week. I guess he figured that if he just left me alone, that would be one less thing for him to be nervous about come game day. If he spent much time discussing things with me, I am sure he would get no sleep leading into the game.*

*"Spike always said your name twice, so when he would ask me a question like, 'Hey, Bill, Bill, they got a couple a double barrel studs over thar on dat Aggie defense, how we gonna git after 'em?' I would come back with, 'How can I eat this soup without a carburetor?' The look on his face was always priceless as he would turn around and walk off. Before he would get out of earshot, I would tell him, 'Don't worry about the mule, Coach, just load the wagon.' Still to this day I don't think he ever heard the second part. I wish now I would have given him a straight answer because he finally quit asking me and it will always be anyone's good fortune to carry on a conversation with Spike Dykes.*

*"There was a time, though, when Spike put me in a head-lock. Don't let the Santa Claus physique fool you. He is power-ful strong. I just finished my rookie year in the NFL and came back to watch some spring practices. I was standing in the stands by the equipment room on the South end of the stadium, look-ing out over the field. Coach Dykes spotted me and walked behind the drill, into the end zone, to say hey. He waddled over (Coach had put on a few pounds that off season) and yelled out, 'Hey, Bill, Bill, good to see you. Come on down and gitcha a close-up look, if ya ain't scared.' I yelled back at him, loud enough for everyone to hear, 'Hell, Coach, I ain't scared, I'm just hungry. Ain't had nothin' to eat all day. If you'll give me one of them Snickers bars I know you got stashed in that jacket I'll be right down.' The whole team was laughing then. I headed down*

*to the field, got to the end zone and Coach came in for what I thought was a big hug. As soon as he got his hands on me, the next thing I knew I was in a headlock, squealing for mercy. Trust me when I say this, Spike Dykes always gets the last word."*

# Chapter 14

# 1994

## Breakthroughs and Breakdowns

No. 1-ranked Nebraska came to Lubbock for the second game of the 1994 season. I felt that the game was closer than the score (42-16) indicated. Of course, that's not a very close score as it is. But our fans deserved a chance to see good teams and that was the case there.

We stayed close to Oklahoma (losing 17-11) the next week, and two weeks later fell narrowly, 23-17, to the No. 10-ranked Texas A&M. They beat us right at the end of the game.

Our habit of losing close games again was countered slightly by our other habit of finishing the season strongly. We won four straight, including a massive game at home against Texas, to get right on the lip of the cup of a Southwest Conference championship. The title was ours alone if we beat Texas Christian University at their place on Nov. 25.

They beat us 24-21 in one of the most heartbreaking losses in all my years, and it felt like everything we were doing was back to ground zero. Pat Sullivan was coaching them and they had a terrific game plan. We couldn't stop them when we had to.

I can say this without fear of overstating it, we got out-coached. They did a couple things we just could not stop. I felt that we had better players and we had everything to play for as we were going for the outright conference championship. We didn't respond well to the challenge. Even when it looked like we had the game finally wrestled out of their control, the Horned Frogs got the ball and moved down the field to beat us.

We still got the Cotton Bowl bid, as five conference teams had 5-3 records in league play, but that TCU game was not one any of us were going to soon forget.

## Cotton Bowl Disaster

What could have been one of our biggest moments turned into our most embarrassing defeat, a 55-14 drubbing by Southern California in the Cotton Bowl following the 1994 season. We hadn't been to a Cotton Bowl since 1939 and we sold more tickets than any participating team ever sold. They said that 60,000 Texas Tech fans were in the stadium that day, which meant we had a hard time hiding once this thing started going badly. Shortly before the Cotton Bowl that year, Reverend Billy Graham had a huge revival in the stadium. One of my so-called friends noted that the folks in the stands were saying, "Oh my God!" as much when we played as they were when Billy Graham was preachin.'

It was a terrible feeling to go from such great excitement to such disappointment. You could really feel the momentum building for us. This was going to be the hump game for us, this was going to truly elevate the program. I don't think we ever had better preparation for a game, or were in a better frame of mind.

We had reason to believe we could do well against the Trojans; we were No. 10 in the nation in scoring defense and had held our previous five opponents to 47 combined points.

Although the Trojans were not that impressive all season, being ranked 21st in the country, they were unbelievably talented. They had Keyshawn Johnson at receiver, Rob Johnson at quarterback and tackle Tony Boselli over on the left side of the line. You might say we had a little trouble staying close to Keyshawn as he caught eight passes for 222 yards and three touchdowns.

Fans had hardly been seated when we were out of the game. It was 28-0 at the end of the first period and 34-0 at the half. The snowball kept growing and the Trojans were up 48-0 before we finally scored. Do you have any concept of how LONG a game feels when you're down by four touchdowns in the first period? Especially playing in front of 60,000 fans who forked over good money to see you make them proud?

It was like having the blood drained out of your body. We couldn't have won a high school game. One positive, though, was our support. Our following made us attractive to bowls, and that can help make you a big-time player in the postseason.

# Very Coordinated

One development that made an enormous difference in the Southern California Trojans was the firing of their defensive coordinator after the regular season and replacing him before the Cotton Bowl. Hard to believe, but they entirely changed their defense for that game. They went from a very passive to very aggressive scheme. Total change. And everything we prepared for was suddenly invalid.

# Chapter 15

# Health

## Chicken-Fried Diet

Nobody ever asked me to endorse any of those fitness centers or weight-loss products, which is kind of funny because I know I've lost over 10,000 pounds. Moderation has never been my deal. I just get to eating and eating and I don't stop until it's gone; I have no discipline in that regard.

Then I'd get real fat, of course, and spend the next six months trying to lose some of the blubber. That means I fluctuate way too much. Sometimes I'll go up or down 20 to 30 pounds. That's not good for anybody, but that's one of my idiosyncrasies.

Favorites? I exist on the four basic food groups: fried chicken, pizza, chicken-fried steak with cream gravy, and ice cream. Fact is, though, if you grow up in West Texas, you get chicken-fried steak before you get pablum.

I know, I know, it's not healthy. I understand the value of working out and how good it is for you. But I've had coaches who worked out every solitary day and I always had to remind them that I've never seen a man jogging with a smile on his face.

# My Cheatin' Heart

I'll admit, this is sort of stupid. In the early summer of 1997, I was about to go to an annual coaches' golf outing to Pebble Beach when I went in for a physical examination. The doctor said, "Man, you are really clogged up, we have to operate on you immediately." I told him I couldn't have heart surgery ... I had a golf outing to go to. Pebble Beach is Pebble Beach, after all.

My heart surgeon, Dr. Don Bricker, said, "Fine, you'll save me having to do the operation because your big fat ass is going to drop dead on some Pebble Beach fairway. You better get you about a five-gallon bucket of nitroglycerin, because you ain't gonna make it to next week without it."

So, I went to golf. Nobody knew about this. Sharon? Well, not entirely. I felt good, never any pain or anything. But when I got back, I realized how important this was, and I called my doctor. As it turned out, he is a big-game hunter who had just gotten a long-awaited permit to shoot some panther or something down in South America. I got through to him that afternoon while he was in the operating room.

"Wait, you can't go off and leave me," I told him. "You said this was an emergency situation."

"Yeah," he said. "Well, it wasn't such an emergency when you wanted to go play golf, now, was it?"

He softened up on me a little, probably not wanting me to expire on his watch. He asked me if I could get into the hospital right then, and he'd do it at that moment. But then he asked if I'd had anything to eat. Well, yeah, I had two chilidogs in the Phoenix airport on the way home. That ruled out the surgery that night (and probably didn't do much for my clogged arteries, either). He said, "Look, if you can get in here at five in the morning, I'll go ahead and do it before I go hunting."

They ended up giving me six bypasses just to get around all the chicken fried steak and cream gravy they found in there.

# Heart Procedure ... Back to Work

In the fall of 1996, doctors saw some test results that suggested I had some arterial blockage. I had no pain and no symptoms, but they had to perform one of those balloon angioplasties.

We beat Oklahoma State, 31-3, on Saturday, and at 6 a.m. Sunday, I was in getting a heart procedure done. Nobody ever knew about it and I was back that afternoon for our workout and films. Didn't miss a day.

You know that old saying about how it doesn't matter if you win or lose ... that doesn't apply to heart surgeries. When they roll you into an operating room, you want that doctor to win, not just do his best.

That's one of the great perks of being a coach—having fine medical care. Those team doctors are always around you and you get physicals with the team every year.

After I retired, I had a blockage of a carotid artery. That's the one that gives you a stroke when it's blocked, and this was very close to 100 percent blocked, with very, very little blood flow. On this one, they operate on your neck and they basically open it up and scoop the stuff out.

The doctor said surviving that one was almost a miracle. So, I've dodged a couple bullets, I'll tell you. What does going through all this mean to you? It obviously reminds you the value of your life and your health, and how precious and fragile it all is.

Son Rick Dykes on Spike's commitment: *"Here's a story that sums up my dad's feelings about commitment. After he had that big carotid artery surgery, he was supposed to be in the hospital until a Friday night. He already had agreed to give a speech to a group of electrical co-op workers in a little-bitty town called Muleshoe, Texas, on Thursday night.*

*"He made me get him out of the hospital after that surgery and drive him to this meeting. He was upset when I wouldn't let him stay for the entire three-hour meeting. He told me that it was important that he be there for those people. At the time, Big 12 Conference coaches had a set fee of $1,000 or so for any speaking engagement. Dad didn't ask for anything. On his way out, they gave him a $20 gift certificate to Outback Steakhouse.*

*"I know that anybody else in the world would have canceled that engagement after a heart surgery. But dad not only felt he had to go, he wanted to spend the entire meeting with those people, too."*

## Commitment

Yeah, I went over to Muleshoe, Texas and spoke … and I guess I liked not to survive it. Rick, my son, gave me hell. But here's the thing; if you say you're going to do something, you need to do it. There are a few things that I felt were important. I never got a letter—good or bad—that I didn't answer. I never got a call I didn't answer. I never had my secretary ask who was calling, because I never wanted it to seem like I'd take somebody's calls and not somebody else's. And if you say you're going to do something for people, you need to be sure to do it.

So, if people ask you to be a speaker, you need to show up. I was probably stupid, but I made that commitment.

# Chapter 16

# 1995

## Our Best Year

While so many good things were happening with our schedule and our overall competitiveness, it had been five years since we had more than six wins in a season. We really felt the importance of raising our production in 1995.

One way to do that, of course, and to legitimize our entire program, would be to play well at Penn State in the opener. We really did play well, although not quite well enough. But we could see we were getting better and getting more consistent.

Why? The talent was better. We had upgraded our schedule and our attendance reflected it. And we were able to start getting some players other teams wanted. With Zebbie Lethridge, Byron Hanspard, Zach Thomas, Marcus Coleman and some other great players, we knew we were headed in the right direction. It added up to nine wins, with two of the losses coming by a combined total of three points. That, friends, is playing pretty competitive football.

## Joe Paterno

We opened up the 1995 season at No. 4-ranked Penn State in front of 96,000 fans. It was a fabulous game in which they kicked a field goal on the last play of the game to edge us 24-23. After the game, coach Joe Paterno came into the press conference and talked at length about how well we played and how good our kids were.

He'll never know it, but he helped the image of our program more that day than just about anything we could have done. He didn't have to, as a narrow win over us might have cost them points in the polls. But he was as gracious as he could be.

That's what makes a lot of those great coaches so special; they are guys who are willing to help somebody on the way up. I couldn't have been more appreciative of how he treated us.

## Biggest Win

Beating the Texas A&M Aggies 14-7 in 1995 on Zach Thomas's interception return was so huge for our program. That was A&M's first conference loss in the 1990s after having won 29 straight.

*Split end Donnie Hart (Stephen Dunn/Getty Images)*

It was an over-capacity crowd and such an exciting turn of events, with Zach intercepting Corey Pullig's pass and returning it for a touchdown to win it in the final minute. It was a third and six, and Zach faked a blitz only to drop back into coverage. Pullig didn't read it and Zach made the pick and ran 23 yards for one of the biggest scores in Tech history.

Zebbie Lethridge, our quarterback, threw for more than 200 yards and the other touchdown we had in the game was a pass to Donnie Hart.

The fans went ballistic, tearing down the goal posts. It was fabulous, beating a top-10 team at home.

Whenever I get together with a bunch of alums, or show up at any kind of football gathering, people still want to talk about that game.

# Zach Thomas

No way around it, Zach Thomas was simply a great college football player. What he's done in the pros is nothing short of phenomenal because he really isn't that great of an athlete. But he was such a leader because the team respected him so much. He barely had to say anything and he had their respect.

Of course, he earned it. The most notable game, of course, was the win over the No. 8 Texas A&M Aggies in Lubbock. That entire week, Zach had a terrible case of the flu, with a 103 fever. It was so bad he couldn't attend classes or practice. He was so diligent, though, that he went to his teachers and informed them of the problem so they could ship his assignments over to him and he could stay current with the books.

In preparation for the game, he sneaked into the football office and picked up every Texas A&M game tape he could find and never left his house for the rest of the week. There he sat, sick as a dog, watching game films all week.

Some teammates kidded him that his mother came down that week to help nurse him. He said, through lips crusted in fever blisters, "I have to give credit to her; if it wasn't for her, I wouldn't be here right now. I'd give her a kiss if my lips weren't so messed up."

Hey, after that interception, I would have gladly puckered up and planted one on Zach's lips. That was a huge play in one of our biggest wins ever.

Former assistant coach Jack Tayrien on Spike's dealing with Zach Thomas: *"Zach got into a fight one time, as I recall, because some guy said something bad to his girlfriend. Because this guy popped off, Zach got himself into a bit of trouble. Coach got him straightened out in a hurry. He told him he can't act like*

*Linebacker Zach Thomas (Al Bello/Getty Images)*

*that because of some chump, and that Zach was going to be a*
*big-time success in pro football, and there would be a long line*
*of guys trying to drag him down.*

*"He told him that he's got to get a lot smarter. And he did.*
*He was a class act, and I know that Coach Dykes really helped*
*him with that."*

## Back to Earth ... at Least to Austin

We had it rolling pretty well, riding a four-game win
streak with a 5-2 record heading into the Texas game on
November 4. But they beat the living dog out of us, just
dominated in every way. There weren't many times that happened to us, but there was no question about this one.
Everything we did failed, and everything they did was perfect. They took no prisoners.

But we won three straight after that to earn a bid in the
Copper Bowl.

## Copper Bowl

If you're a stickler for defense, the 1995 Copper Bowl
might have gone against your grain. But this was one of the
most exciting games ever, and certainly the highest scoring in
the bowl season that year.

With Byron Hanspard rushing for 260 yards and four
touchdowns, and Zebbie Lethridge adding more than 300
yards of total offense, we gained 606 yards against the Air

Force in a 55-41 win. That's a ton of yards against a rushing team like the Air Force.

We got a little fancy in this one, opening with a no-huddle offense featuring four or five wide receivers. Zebbie had a tremendous first half to put us up 31-13, and then Byron took over in the second half to control the tempo of the game.

That helped us get our second nine-win season in our years at Tech. Nine wins against the kind of competition we faced in 1995 is a pretty decent record for just about any school.

It felt good to get back on track in a bowl game. Over our 13 years, we went to six bowls, which was pretty good for Texas Tech. But there's something different about preparing to play in bowls, and I'm not sure there's a magic formula. We went up to watch how coach Tom Osborne had done it at Nebraska, and he made it clear that every team has its own personality and needs to get prepared according to its own nature.

We were in five bowl games the five years I was an assistant at Texas, and every time we did something different.

# Stoney Garland

Thankfully, we never lost a player while I coached at Tech. But we had a tragedy involving one of our best young men—Stoney Garland.

Stoney was a great ball player, a defensive tackle who would have made it in the National Football League. He was a junior-college transfer with a bright future. During the Thanksgiving holiday of 1995, Stoney was in a little fender bender and it whiplashed his neck.

He's a quadriplegic now. The team and the community were more supportive than you could ever believe. It was just a tragic event and a tragic situation that reminds you to be sure to be thankful for all the good things that happen to you every day.

I still see Stoney quite a bit. We do a lot of work trying to help him out. One of the real stories behind this sad event is the enormous strength of Stoney's mother, Debbie Garland. I believe she's the bravest woman on this planet. If there's ever been an angel on Earth, it's Debbie Garland.

She is a single parent who works a couple jobs trying to pay for things. I'll tell you, she's been a real rallying point for people at Texas Tech. She has never been into that poor-me syndrome although she works unbelievable hours. It's going to be a struggle for both Stoney and Debbie.

Stoney has had a tough time, but he's managed to get out and speak to some high schools. He tells them never to take things for granted and don't ever complain about the small things that irritate you. I'll tell you, he's done a wonderful job of sharing his experience with kids. And he's a tough hombre who has never lost his grip. Of course, he's just like his momma … tough, tough, tough people who are fighting hard and never feeling sorry for themselves.

I think they're both inspirations. To me, they're both heroes.

Former athletic director T Jones on Stoney Garland: *"Spike has been at the side of Stoney and his mother every moment that it was possible. He has stayed in constant contact with them and simply would not forget them when he left. He's very loyal as a friend and as a coach. He's one of those people who you know will be there in tough times."*

# Chapter 17

# Characters

## Getting His Goat

Strong safety Reagan Bownds might not be recognized as a two-sport star in a lot of states, but in Texas, if you're a football player who is also a world champion goat roper, that's big stuff.

He was also everything you could ever want in a college student/athlete. He was a terrific hitter and a heads-up player who was also a Phi Beta Kappa student.

You can take the kid out of Eldorado, Texas, but you can't take Eldorado out of the kid. Bownds got his degree with high honors and then took a job as a ranch foreman 65 miles from the nearest town.

He was just the darnedest guy you ever saw. But you sure didn't hear much out of him. I'll bet he didn't say 200 words the whole time he was at Tech. Maybe he talked to the goats some, but he didn't share much with the rest of us.

*Strong safety Reagan Bownds (Stephen Dunn/Getty Images)*

## The Curious Bam

I can tell you this—not a sweeter guy was ever born than Bam Morris. They don't come any better. He's such a neat guy and I've got tremendous respect for him.

If he spent time with Billy Graham, he would have become the greatest preacher ever. If he spent time with Billy the Kid, he could become a great bank robber. I just loved him, which makes me sad about some of the things that have happened with him and the law.

I think he found himself with the wrong crowd and got in some of the wrong places at the wrong times. He's got a terrific momma who is an unbelievable person, but when you're young, you have to learn to make good decisions, and that's been a hard thing for him. I don't think he used very good judgment on when to say yes and when to say no.

None of that changes the way I feel about him, and I'm sorry things happened. It doesn't mean I condone anything he's done, but I also don't think he needs to be damned for life because of the troubles he's had. If you know him, there's an awful lot to Bam ... there really is.

Rick Dykes on Bam Morris: *"I know dad loved Bam. But almost everybody did. He was such a funny kid. And was he a character. When he was new to the program, he came into the room where we were having a running backs meeting. He was a very highly recruited player, but he was still one of the new guys in a group of veterans. This one meeting, Bam had terrible gas. And we were in a very small room. I mean, it was one after another. Anthony Lynn, one of our great players and an upper-classman, said, 'Bam, if you fart one more time, I'm gonna come back there and MAKE you stop.' Bam looked at him and said, 'Anthony, I can't stop; my momma told me that if I didn't get rid of those gas bubbles, they might get in my blood and go up to my heart and kill me.' Everybody laughed so hard it took 30 minutes to get back to the meeting."*

# Toughest Ever

One guy from Tech's past established a standard for toughness that would be pretty difficult for modern players to match. E.J. Holub was a Tech All-American and a professional player so talented he's the only one ever to start on defense in one Super Bowl and on offense in another.

E.J. has been a great and loyal Texas Tech supporter over the years. He's one of those guys who really paid the price to play football. He's pretty beat up and I'm sure he's in a lot of pain. He had more than 20 knee operations. When he got replacements for his knees, he got two inches taller.

People who played against him in the NFL have told me that he's just the toughest there ever was ... nobody like him.

He's a character, too. He's an old cowboy. He rode his horse into a bar in Dallas one time. Right up on the stage. He's a hoot, and some kind of great guy.

Former Tech great E.J. Holub on his best Spike story: *"I pulled a good one on him one day. They were having spring practice one day wearing just helmets, shorts and jerseys. I talked to an equipment manager and got a big size-8 helmet that could spin all the way around my head, and a jersey and some shorts. I told him not to say anything to Spike, but I went out and got in the drills with the linebackers.*

*"Here I was wearing a pair of Hush Puppy shoes, and had those scarred-up knees of mine sticking out from under these shorts. Some of the other coaches saw me and just put their hands over their mouths. The linebackers were doing drills where they make contact with the tight ends coming off the line. In my day, you could just give them a hand-shiver shot to the head ... so I did a couple of those and the coaches told me I better get out of there and go see Spike.*

*"I had my head down so he couldn't really see me, and even with those shoes on and those scarred knees sticking out, Spike didn't figure out who I was. He says, 'What can I do for you, son?' I said, 'Coach, I think I've got to go to class.' I raised my head and he saw who it was and I thought he was going to kick me in the [groin]. It was hilarious."*

# Dave Parks

The San Francisco 49ers drafted Dave Parks out of Texas Tech in the first round in 1964, and he had a terrific career for them. When I got to Tech, it seemed like he was estranged from the program for some reason. I saw him after I became head coach and I asked him if he'd come up during spring ball and watch us practice.

It was really nice. He did and he got back into the family and got interested in our little program. He's the most loyal good guy there's ever been. I don't think he missed a game, home or away. He was a real good friend to our program.

# Chapter 18

# 1996

## Big 12, Big Time

Getting into the Big 12 Conference was a crucial development for Texas Tech. Now we were lodge brothers with the likes of Nebraska, Oklahoma, Kansas State, Colorado, etc. Of course, that only upped the ante for us, too, but the rewards were worth the cost of going out almost every week against top opposition.

It didn't start out that great, however, as we lost our first game in the new conference to Kansas State, 21-14, in Manhattan, Kansas. We got down to their goal line and couldn't score. It was one of those deals that breaks your heart, but it happens.

We beat up on Oklahoma State the next week, but got last-driven again on the road against a quality opponent, Georgia, after that. We were ahead 12-8 in front of 73,000 fans and they executed a perfect deep ball to beat us.

*Quarterback Zebbie Lethridge (Stephen Dunn/Getty Images)*

No. 5-ranked Nebraska came to town and we once again topped 50,000 in attendance. The fans got a good game, if not the win, as we were in it 17-10 before falling 24-10.

That was the first in a series of three games against powerhouses and rivals ... Nebraska, Texas A&M and Texas. We only won one of those games, but all three were extremely competitive.

We were down at College Station playing Texas A&M in the fourth quarter when Zebbie Lethridge ran a little naked bootleg, throwback pass to Sammy Morris, who caught it and turned it into an 81-yard game-winning touchdown.

It was a great call. My son, Rick, was our offensive coordinator, and he had very strong feelings that play was going to work. He had set that thing up and was just waiting for the right time to spring it on them. His patience paid off, and it was a great win for us.

Byron Hanspard was brilliant once again, with 198 rushing yards on 41 carries. Forty-one carries ... that's a day's work. It was the 14th game in a row that he rushed for more than 100 yards.

Texas edged us 38-32, but we still finished the regular season with seven wins and an Alamo Bowl berth against a powerful Iowa team.

# Don't Remember the Alamo

It was big stuff at Texas Tech to qualify for our fourth consecutive bowl. Bowls were getting easier to get into, but we also were playing a lot tougher schedules, which added to the difficulty of reaching bowl eligibility in wins.

None of that mattered much when we lined up against Iowa, though. We just got shelled. It was ugly. They had a vaunted running attack and were so big and physical we just could not stop them. They lined up and put the Big Ten mash on us with those big linemen and big backs.

That little returner, Tim Dwight, who had such a nice NFL career, just ran all over us. He ran a punt back on us. Actually, everything they did worked, and we were blanked 27-0.

# Chapter 19

# Unsung Elements

## More Than Ankle Tapers

Trainers, along with strength coaches, are the ones who get to know the players better than the coaches do. They're with the players at times when they drop their guard. They don't have to protect themselves as much as they do around coaches, and they're not afraid to say things to trainers. It makes trainers very good sounding boards for the players. And it allows the training staff to know far more about the state of mind of the team than a coach will ever know.

Ken Murray was our trainer for a number of years, and he was fantastic. And so was the woman who took over after him, Natalie Steadman. These two managed that difficult balancing job that is a trainer's life. They know that coaches want players back on the field as soon as possible, but they also know how important it is to be cautious with injuries.

I told our staff that if they want to be trainers, then they should go get their degrees in training. Until then, whatever the trainer says about a player is the law. That's the way it was always going to be. If they say a guy can't play, then he isn't going to play, and the coach is going to keep his mouth shut about it.

Now, it's natural to ask if there's something else we can do to help the guy along ... go to a chiropractor or get massages or extra therapy, whatever.

So, the trainers and the strength coaches are part of those unsung components of a successful program—equipment managers, too. And I'm not so sure that there was anybody more valuable to me in all the time I was at Texas Tech than my secretary, Patty Ross. She lived and died with those kids, and they were comfortable telling her things they'd never dream of telling me. She put up with so much from me, answering all those calls. She is the most loyal human being in the whole world. She was really something special.

## Good Scouts

If you wake up every morning and you're bigger and faster and stronger and more talented than the next guy, football is going to be fun for you. That's natural. But if you're not so big or fast or strong, it might be a struggle just to hang in there.

The men who occupied the scout squads are usually in that second category. It's a tough job, it's an anonymous job, but it's not thankless ... because we thanked them as much as we could for their important contributions.

These guys go out there every single solitary day and practice just as long and hard as everybody else, but have little chance of getting onto the field on Saturday. If they don't do their jobs during the week, chances are we're going to end up with a loss. They're that important. Without them, you have no hope of fielding a successful team.

One of our all-time best scout-team guys was a Phi Beta Kappa student named Rudy Renda. He was a walk-on for us who was the greatest scout team player in the whole world. What set him apart was his attitude, and the importance he attached to his performance every day. If you've got people hitting you and grabbing your jersey all day, it can get pretty depressing. But Rudy Renda never gave less effort than any of the star players we had.

We really tried to let them know how valuable they were to us; we tried to include them in everything. And when it came time to hand out letters, we never forgot their value to the team.

## Don't Blame the Horse

The tradition of the Masked Rider is unique in college football. It goes back a long way and it means a lot to Red Raider football fans. Every year, a Masked Rider is selected among some very gifted horsemen and women. It's a very prestigious position at Tech, and I think it's one of the best traditions in college football. After scores, the horse and rider circle the field.

The part that visiting teams don't care for much is the way the horse rides past their bench. Officials were always a little edgy about the horse running somebody down, and opposing coaches were always complaining. Absolutely none of them shared our admiration for the Masked Rider.

Tech is a tough place for people to play. And if you go someplace and have a bad game, the first thing you're going to do is blame that poor horse. I'll tell you, that horse got lots of nasty looks over the years.

*The Masked Horse Rider (Sean Meyers/Icon SMI)*

## Flying Tortillas

In the mid-'90s, for no apparent reason, tortillas just started flying out of the stands.

Fans just started hurling tortillas onto the field whenever they felt like it.

It's a pretty untidy tradition and one you're not real proud of because it makes such a mess. But I promise you those other teams don't like coming in there and getting nailed all game by flying tortillas.

The first time I saw them flying around, I didn't know what in the world was happening. Of course, before long, it got to be a big thing and made a real mess. It's not something anybody was real proud of, but those kids were just having fun. The administration was never happy about it. And I had to discourage it.

To tell the truth, yeah, I was sorta amused by the whole thing. I wasn't supposed to be, and, of course, I was supposed to support the administration position, but it really was pretty entertaining.

# Men in Stripes

Here's something you might not hear a coach say in public: I love officials. These guys are such a big part of the game, and some of the best friends I have are officials. You couldn't play the game without them.

One time I went out there and got on one of them and called him everything I could think of. But he shut me up, pronto. He said, "Coach, if I were officiating as badly as your team is playing, I'd get my little ass right over to the sidelines and keep my mouth shut." He had a point and I buttoned up.

Coaches and fans have to remember that these guys are human, and I've had them come back to me and tell me they missed calls. I appreciated that. Fans also don't know what a special group of guys they are. They love the game so much. The crew may be a doctor, a lawyer, a teacher, a millionaire contractor, whatever, but the most important thing in their lives are those games.

It's really a heckuva fraternity and I admire the heck out of them. Yes, we've had officials who probably cost us games. We've probably had some win some for us, too. On balance, those guys are a big part of what the game is today and they really do a terrific job.

# Brain Crew

For anybody still laboring under the misconception that football players are a gang of dummies, I submit the achievements of five seniors I had in my last year at Tech. They all lived together and two of them were walk-on players. Three of them never made anything but A's and two of them had one B.

The five were Rob Peters, Kyle Shipley, Rudy Renda, Reagan Bownds, and Keith Cockrum. Keith was the national Burger King Scholar-Athlete of the Year.

Former quarterback Billy Joe Tolliver on a special teammate: *"A man I played with at Texas Tech taught the meaning of wearing that Double T on your helmet to me. His name is Ryan Strong. Ryan Strong hailed from Amarillo and spent his youth dreaming of playing for the Red Raiders. He ended up walking on at Texas Tech and was given the duty of being the center for the quarterbacks in all of our drills. Oh, he still had to do all his offensive linemen work, but we had his services when we needed them.*

*"This doesn't seem like much but when you consider that besides all the O-Line work that he had to do, he must have snapped easily 500,000 balls over his five-year career. It was grunt work, nothing at all glamorous. But to the quarterbacks there was no one on our team any more important to us than 'Cat Daddy' Strong. The sacrifices he made for the good of the team just so we could maintain the timing between center exchange and the route being thrown should not go unnoticed. He gave of himself every day and never complained about not getting his shot at competing for a starter or back-up role. It wasn't because he was satisfied just being on the team. It was because he was a selfless man and did what had to be done.*

*"I thank you, Ryan Strong, for teaching all of us what it is to give of yourself and for showing me, early on, what it means to call yourself a Texas Tech Red Raider."*

# Chapter 20

# 1997

## Peyton's Place

This was the scenario we outlined for recruits. We opened the 1997 season at Tennessee in front of a crowd that established an NCAA attendance record of more than 106,000. And we did pretty well for the first three quarters before the Vols' great quarterback, Peyton Manning, unleashed his full repertoire.

You'd think you had him sacked, but he was so strong you couldn't bring him down. You'd try to blitz him to get in his face, but he was so smart he'd read it and get rid of the ball with his quick release, burning you almost every time. He made it easy to see why he's so great in the NFL. He was well coached, with an innate ability to play the position.

They beat us 52-17, but that was hardly the most disheartening loss of the early season.

# Mean Green

Okay, you lose at Tennessee in front of a crowd that was more than half the size of Lubbock. That's understandable, especially with Peyton Manning at the controls.

But then to lose at home to North Texas is the kind of thing that killed us. The Mean Green deserve all the credit in the world and I deserved all the blame. They lined up and beat us; they played hard and did everything they needed to do to win. But that's the sort of thing that can really shake up the fans.

# Mr. Rogers

Nebraska shut us out in 1997, but they were the No. 2-ranked team in the nation when we played them. So it's fair to say they treated a lot of opponents that way. But the next week against the Texas A&M Aggies provided a very rectifying—not to mention dramatic—win for us.

As big as this 16-13 win was for us, it was more crucial for place kicker Tony Rogers. Rogers had lost his job the previous season when he missed four of five field goals against Kansas State. But starting kicker Jason Greaser was injured, thrusting Rogers back into action.

Rogers made three field goals that day, and the final one was a 47-yarder with 19 seconds remaining. It bounced off the left upright and fell through. Beautiful … simply beautiful. If you make a hole in one after bouncing it off a bunker rake, it still counts as an ace.

That kick jump-started the second half of the season for us, as we lost narrowly to a No. 13-ranked Kansas State team, beat Texas on the road and also beat a top 25 Oklahoma State team on the road before losing 32-21 to Oklahoma.

That little finishing surge helped get us off to a great start in 1998.

# Raw Deal

Zebbie Lethridge and a fullback named Rod Hobbs had gone shopping in a mall in Lubbock. As the story goes, when they got ready to leave one of the stores, Rod challenged Zebbie to a race to the car. Off they went, running at full speed.

Security guards grabbed them and accused them of shoplifting. It was the biggest bogus thing that ever happened. They had a receipt for everything in their bags, but the police were called anyway. Anybody who ever knew Zebbie knew he would never do that. He came from a great family right there in Lubbock. Of course, his picture was all over the front of the paper.

For some reason, even without evidence, they wouldn't drop the charges. Finally, after an extended period of time, he sued them for false arrest and won hands down. He got a nice payday out of it, but it was a real headache for everybody.

Zebbie was a great leader and a great person, and he was one of those guys that you could stake your life on the fact that he hadn't done anything wrong.

# Chapter 21

# Off the Field

## Life Skills

Players come to college from remarkably diverse backgrounds. Some are much better prepared for the challenges of being away from home and being on their own than others might be.

So, one thing we used to do was have a "class" on Thursday nights with just me and the team. Period. No other coaches; I gave them the night off to go home and see their wives.

I'm sure a lot of the players rolled their eyes at my stories, but I tried to explain some things about life to them. We didn't even talk about football. I felt it was important to share with them some things that they needed to know.

I talked about what it means to represent the university. They represent more than themselves; it's as if they're carrying a flag for the school and being an ambassador for a lot of things that some people consider sacred. No one ever wants to put himself in a position to tarnish the things we stand for.

We discussed how to deal with the media, how they have a job to do and how they can help you if you know how to work with them. If they ask you a question, just be honest and respectful. Sometimes ugly is ugly and you can't paint it up to make it pretty.

Some of the players felt there might be better ways to spend some time on Thursday evenings, but I know some of them also appreciated the message that was being shared with them.

# Red Raiders in the Community

Our players were terrific about getting out and volunteering and helping around Lubbock. A lot of players gave their time going to junior high schools and elementary schools all over the region to speak. These kids really gave back and never turned down an invitation. They were aware of the kinds of troubles kids can get into and all the things that can get a good kid sidetracked. So many of them were good counselors and role models. I know they were positive influences on a lot of young people.

We had a strong Fellowship of Christian Athletes group, too. Our great back, Bryon Hanspard, was a preacher, and I went to hear him conduct several Sunday services. The public didn't always notice all the good works of these young men, but the community appreciated it ... and so did I. I was really proud of these guys and how they recognized how important they could be in the lives of others.

Former quarterback Billy Joe Tolliver on the Tech experience: *"You have to begin with the fact that it is not just the team or the athletic department. The entire Red Raider Nation raises the child to be a man. The city of Lubbock embraces you. It's the West Texas way of life. It is easy to grow as a human being just by following the example of the West Texan. They live their lives steeped in honor, loyalty. courage, commitment, and they say what they mean and mean what they say. They are West Texas proud and Red Raider loud. Parents should feel comfort in sending their child to Texas Tech, because in Lubbock you've got a friend and family. They certainly helped shape the mold of this country boy."*

# Chapter 22

# 1998

## Hot Start

For years we lost early games we should have won, or failed to sustain our momentum on a weekly basis. Finally, through the first six weeks of the 1998 season, we got it together and kept it going. We didn't play many great clubs, but the sad thing about the streak is that it could have been considerably longer.

We lost three straight to top 20 teams—Colorado, Texas A&M and Missouri—by a total of 11 points. Colorado scored right at the end to beat us, and it looked like we scored right at the end of the 17-10 loss to Texas A &M. The pass from Rob Peters to Donnie Hart was disallowed because officials said he was out of bounds. From my standpoint, it was a very questionable call, and I think we just plain got hosed on that one.

We should have beaten Missouri, too, but they did a great job of controlling the time of possession and we just

*Quarterback Rob Peters (Stephen Dunn/Getty Images)*

couldn't get the ball away from them and dropped the game 28-26.

# We 'Rob' Texas

Quarterback Rob Peters had been injured leading up to the Texas showdown in November of 1998, but when he took the field against the Longhorns, he put together one of the greatest displays of determination I'd seen. He simply refused to let us lose that game.

We scored 22 points in the last quarter to win 42-35 in coach Mack Brown's first year at Texas. Rob had a career-high 322 passing yards, with 250 of those coming in the second half. He also scored the game-winner on a sneak.

*Running back Ricky Williams (Stephen Dunn/Getty Images)*

Our running back Ricky Williams outgained Texas's more acclaimed running back Ricky Williams by a 148-141 count.

We lost a close one, 20-17, at Oklahoma in the final regular-season game, but we still got seven wins and a bid to the Independence Bowl. Of course, once we got there, a darned good Mississippi team just lined up and took it to us, scoring three touchdowns in the fourth quarter to beat us 35-21.

# Chapter 23

# Opposing Coaches

## Adjusting Our Goals

Texas Christian University coach Jim Wacker was one of the most positive people I've ever seen; happy and bubbly and funny all the time. A lot of coaches, if you beat them, they'll blame everybody but themselves—the officials, the circumstances, anything.

Not Jim. I had a little fun with Jim one year when they came to Lubbock. It was the first year they narrowed the goal posts, and before the game I said, "Jim, I'm sure sorry, but we didn't have the money to get some new goal posts, so we just left the ones we had and told everybody they're new and they're the right size." I was just foolin' with him, of course.

Jim was all "Gosh" and "Golly" and "What are we going to do?" I told him that since it wasn't going to hurt either team more than the other, we needed to just keep it between ourselves. He wasn't sure, but he went along with it. They beat us that game and I'm almost sorry the outcome didn't come down to a last-second field goal ... might have been fun to see how Jim addressed that.

# A Vote for Osborne

Before he got into politics, Tom Osborne, of course, was hugely successful as Nebraska's head coach. People should know that he was not just immensely capable, but equally gracious.

He didn't have to be, but Tom Osborne was extremely helpful to me when I first became a head coach. We weren't in the same league at the time, but he didn't have to be so open and sharing and thoughtful as he was.

Even when the Big 12 Conference was being formed and we were going to end up in the same league, he was still

*Tom Osborne (Brian Bahr/Getty Images)*

extremely helpful. One year I wanted to see how he prepared his teams for bowls because they were always so successful. I called him and he allowed me to come up for three or four days to watch their preparations. He certainly could have been excused if he'd said, "Aw, we're really busy now." But he didn't; he was very welcoming and very, very gracious.

That, friends, is a class act.

# Spike-ism

Some typical fans think you've got to have some kind of hatred for an opposing coach. They don't understand that some of the best friends I've ever had are opposing coaches. Brigham Young University's LaVell Edwards became a great friend and we'd go off to clinics together all the time. You travel in the same circles and you get to know these guys. They're also some of the few people in the world who understand what you're going through on a day-to-day basis.

Former BYU coach LaVell Edwards on Spike's persona: *"He puts on this country bumpkin act while all the time he's usually about three steps ahead of you … very shrewd, very smart. And he doesn't change whether he's in New York City or West Texas. He's a tremendous individual and a great friend. He is what he is, and he's one of the most loyal people there's ever been in the business.*

*"In the first place, he's a great football coach. But more than that, in terms of being the right person for a job … he was a perfect fit for Texas Tech. He knew the way things operate there, and he did a great job of recruiting to Lubbock, and then of coaching the guys he got.*

*"His teams were always extremely well coached and fundamentally ready to play. You look at the record he had against Texas and Texas A&M, and it's amazing. So much of it was his approach: He'd give you that down-home attitude and the next thing you know, you were getting out-smarted and out-coached. I thought the job he did there was truly remarkable."*

# Chapter 24

# Knock Wood

## Very Superstitious

Yeah, I've got a few superstitions; they came from my mother. She ingrained them in me and they're not something to mess with. To me, there are a few things you just do not do. You certainly never cross where a black cat crossed. I've driven 15 miles out of the way because the black cat thing is instant bad luck. I don't care if I'm 400 miles from the nearest human being; I'm not driving there. I know it's a bunch of baloney; I know it means you're insecure or something, but I still do it. These things are omens from beyond.

When I was coaching at Coahoma, we won about four games in a row and we decided it was because of our socks and clothes. So the coaches didn't change them. Didn't wash them. Just wore them for four weeks. What did my wife Sharon think? She was so busy changing diapers at the time she didn't notice the smell.

Heads-up pennies, now, those are GOOD luck, and you've got to pick them up whenever you see one. Before one game that I remember, at Tech, there were so many heads-up pennies in the parking lot it took me about half an hour to get to the locker room. Man, I knew we were going to have some good luck in that game.

Son Rick Dykes on Spike's superstitions: *"Trying to have a little fun with my dad's superstitions, one time we spread around dozens of heads-up pennies all over the parking lot before one game. That kept him busy."*

## You Gonna Finish That?

The players always accused me of stealing their food. They would kind of get all protective with their arms wrapped around their plates when they saw me coming. I'll grant you that I wouldn't get my own plate for the pregame meal because, mostly, I was dieting. I got a reputation for just "grazing," walking past players and grabbing a French fry, or whatever, but I don't think I was that bad.

I really was a stickler for having players eat what they were served, though. And I kept an eye on them. If I saw them throwing away a big plate of uneaten food, it really bothered me. I guess it was my upbringing, but I really believe it is wrong to waste food when there are people starving to death all over the world.

# Cheek Candy

Yes, dang it, I used chewing tobacco on the sidelines. I know it's not very attractive or sanitary. But I tried to do it discreetly; I never had a huge wad in there.

And I'd like to note that I never once spit on a kid nor official nor alum nor member of the media. Even though I might have been tempted on occasion.

Friend Ronnie Flowers on being "adopted" by Spike: *"I've been a poor boy all my life. I ran into Coach Dykes when I was a shipping and receiving clerk in a sporting goods store in Lubbock. When I met him, he treated me like I was one of the owners of the place. We became good friends. Here's what kind of guy he is: He took me to Pebble Beach to play in a coaches' golf tournament. I broke my watch and I mentioned that I felt naked without one. When I got home from the trip, he sent me a watch. It was one of those nice, engraved ones from one of Tech's bowl appearances. That's the way he treats everybody, whether they're the clerk at the 7-11 or the president of the United States."*

# Alums, Boosters and Joe Fan

Alums are the same everywhere… they want to win every game. At Texas Tech, they were a great bunch of strong fans. We used to have a luncheon every Thursday that was always packed. We showed them the films of the previous game and gave them a chance to ask a lot of questions like: "Aw, Spike, why did you throw the ball on third and four?"

Anything they asked, I'd tell them. What was nice is that it was a chance for them to vent any frustrations they had by going to the horse's mouth for the answers. It also gave them a nice chance to share in the wonderful emotions after victories.

What is important to remember, especially at a place like Texas Tech, is that all the fans aren't the heavy hitters with the 50-yard-line seats or buildings on campus named after them. Certainly, those people are important, but we also needed the guy who figures out a way to buy a ticket on Saturday because he just loves watching Tech football.

I tried to make sure that Tech football was accessible to anybody who wanted to be a part of it. Those folks are the real hardcore support of most programs. I know we loved them at Texas Tech.

# Whither College Football

I like the direction in which college football is headed. Frankly, I've never been a follower of pro football; I just never enjoyed watching it that much. You can enjoy and appreciate the great players, of course, but everybody does the same thing every Sunday. Same plays, same formations, same defenses ... it gets boring.

I'm also not sure the effort is always there in the pro game. I shouldn't say that because I've never been a part of it, but it just doesn't look like everybody is always playing that hard on every play. You don't have to worry about that in a college game, or even a high school game.

College has a nice variety, no doubt about it. And there's nothing like it on Saturday afternoons with the great crowds, the great traditions and the great bands. I don't think there's anything like it in the whole world.

We opened up at Tennessee in 1997 and there were more than 106,000 fans there. The year we opened at Penn State, there were 15,000 people who showed up without tickets just to stand around outside the stadium and be NEAR the action. Now, that's being a real fan.

The atmosphere is so genuine because college football is such an ingrained part of college life. Nobody is going to argue that college is a place to get an education, but there's a lot more to it than that. Football is a part of all that, it helps make the experience complete.

Maybe this is veering off toward being corny, but I truly believe that the American spirit of enthusiasm and commitment and sacrifice and loyalty are things you don't get out of math books. These are important parts of our country's heritage and I think you get much of that from football.

Of course, you get the occasional player who embarrasses you, but I'm sure there are some engineering students who get in trouble, too.

# Big Money

College football has turned into a pretty lucrative job for some folks, no doubt about it. With the Bowl Championship Series and television contracts, there's obviously a lot of money out there to be had.

But that's not the reason for the game. The reason for the game is for, say, the University of Texas to have a chance to compete against Texas A&M and give the fans and students from both sides something to cheer about. That's the important part.

I don't worry about the big contracts some coaches have landed, either. If you look at CEOs of big corporations, they're making huge money. I think those coaches who run great and successful programs, who serve their universities well, are to be commended and compensated.

Steve Spurrier was making $2 million a year at Florida and some people raised a stink about it, but the stadium was always full and the Florida athletic department and the Florida prestige were greatly enhanced by him being there. You've got to remember, too, it's pretty hard to stay on top. You've got constant scrutiny every single step of the way. You're getting judged every day.

There are probably a lot of coaches who aren't getting nearly what they deserve, in fact. I think you go by whatever the traffic will bear. Of course, a big contract and a bad season can conspire to get you fired, too.

# The Juice

Programs that run into problems with steroids may just not be keeping their eyes open enough. I don't believe people can do that stuff undetected if you have your antennas up. There's way too much change in people. Of course, you can close your eyes if you want.

I think when you look at it, there's, what, 100 and some Division I-A football teams. When you look at maybe 10,000 participants at that level, well, there's going to be some guys who are out of step. If you take 10,000 of anything, there's going to be some who are not as honest as the others.

## Limited Resources

In the early stages of the Big 12 Conference, as far as budget was concerned, we were D.A.L. … dead-ass-last. So what?

Money and resources, all that stuff is in the eyes of the beholder. Either you wake up and decide to do your best every day or you find 43 things to bitch about. I hated bitching. If I started bitching, then all of a sudden I've got 10 assistants who would be bitching too.

## Spike-ism

No, you can't sit around and giggle or act like it's grade-school recess all the time. But you can have fun with football. If you don't have fun, why play it? You could probably go across the street and get a job at 7-11 to make enough to pay your tuition. Why go through all the pain if it's no fun? Football's tough; there's blisters and there's tears and sometimes there's crutches. So, you've got to make the most out of it and have fun whenever you can.

Former assistant coach Tommy McVay on Spike's generosity: *"I was director of football operations and sometimes we didn't have much in the way of resources. I saw Spike use his own credit card to pick up office supplies for the staff when we ran out. He used to let his assistants split the money for the football camps, and didn't keep any for himself.*

*"It wasn't always pretty; sometimes he'd come out of that office wearing just a pair of gym shorts. It was a sight to behold.*

*But he didn't care much. We always said he was the kind of guy to give you the shirt off his back."*

Former assistant coach Jack Tayrien on Spike's manner of dress: *"Spike used to tell me that he never paid much attention to the way he dressed because people just got to know him and expected him to look a little disheveled. He used to pull up in front of a recruit's house wearing a sweatshirt and jeans. He'd stop at every little convenience store on the way down and he'd have a hot dog and a snack and get that stuff, and a little juice, all over his shirt.*

*"He'd pull up to the recruit's house in these little-bitty towns and I'd ask him if he intended to get dressed. He'd whip off that sweatshirt and change shirts in the street. Neighbors would be looking out the window at him and there he was stripping down. He usually put on a coat and looked pretty nice by the time he went in.*

*"On one trip to Houston, he was going to speak at a high school banquet and I showed up and was going to stay with him at the hotel. Spike had been on a diet and had lost a good bit of weight. Sharon had packed his bags for him, and he had a green coat and gray slacks that fit when he weighed in the 240s. Problem was, he was about 210 at the time.*

*"Spike got a safety pin from the front desk and used it to cinch up the back of his pants. So, he was in pinned-up gray pants, with a baggy green jacket, brown shoes and a blue tie. I finally gave up and gave him my black tie and my black shoes. Here's the bad part, I had to wear all of Spike's hand-me-downs and I was a mess."*

# Beg Your Pardon

Sure, I dress casually. Life is casual unless you make it complicated. I mean, I don't go to church in blue jeans, but dressing up never was at the top of my priority list. I'm not proud of it, I just always sorta wore whatever was there.

Son Rick Dykes on Spike's attire: *"I've seen him come out of his office wearing gym shorts and nothing else. No shirt ... barefoot. It's a real sight. Really, though, he understood that in some homes in West Texas if you showed up in a three-piece suit, you would offend somebody. He seemed to have a pretty good sense of what the situation called for."*

# Ten Percent Theory

The way I calculate it, as a coach, you lose about 10 percent of your friends every year. And that's in a good year; attrition is proportional to losing. Especially in high schools. What happens is, if you play one kid at quarterback, the other quarterback's daddy may be on the school board and not fully appreciate your evaluation of personnel. The next thing is maybe you're not throwing the ball much and the parents of the receivers fail to see the wisdom of your offensive scheme.

The same holds true in college, except it's administrators, alums, boosters and the like who are growing weary of your act. What a coach has to realize is that if you worry about that stuff, you shouldn't be coaching.

I promise you this, I never met a coach who didn't do what he thought was best to win every game. You don't win every one, of course, and you make mistakes, too. So, along the way, your personal bandwagon develops more vacancies on an annual basis.

# Chapter 25

# 1999

## The Last Go-Round

I knew heading into the 1999 season that I was going to retire. I had talked to chancellor John Monfort about it, and he had asked me to stay through the NCAA sanctions, and I agreed to do that.

Texas Tech owes a great deal to chancellor Monfort; he had great vision and it was a delight to work for him. We were entirely on the same page that this would be the last season. Very few people knew about it, of course. Sharon knew, but I didn't want to make a big deal out of it. It really wasn't a bittersweet season or anything; there was very little difference. Football at Texas Tech was about the kids, not about me. All I did was drive the bus.

Maybe something was going on, though, because this was the most up and down season we ever had. We beat the good teams and lost to the bad teams. The thing that really killed us—and this is not a valid excuse because it happens a lot in this game—was our injuries. It was the most disheart-ening thing. I don't think we started the same team two weeks in a row all year.

The thing that was a testimony to those kids was that we would lose to North Texas or get hammered by Texas, but they didn't go crawl into a hole, they came out and played hard the next week. That says so much about their character.

# Aggie Upset

We were an unimposing 1-2 when we took on the No. 5-ranked Texas A&M Aggies on October 2, 1999. Sammy Morris had missed the previous two games with a shoulder injury, and we were banged up all over the field.

But we shook up our offense before that game, altering our scheme to make better use of Morris at tailback. The real difference came in terms of emotion, though. The team had a meeting on Friday night before the game, discussing the importance of playing with passion against the Aggies.

They certainly did that, with Morris rushing for 179 yards, giving us our fourth win in five duels against the Aggies. The fans were a bit emotional, too, rushing onto the field and ripping down the goal posts. Hey, they deserved to cut loose.

Former assistant coach Jack Tayrien on Spike's meteor-ological interests: *"Maybe it was how much time he spent on the golf course dealing with those unpredictable West Texas winds that got Spike so concerned about the weather. He always want-ed to know the precise conditions and forecast before every game. It paid off in 1999 when the No. 5 Texas A&M Aggies showed up in Lubbock.*

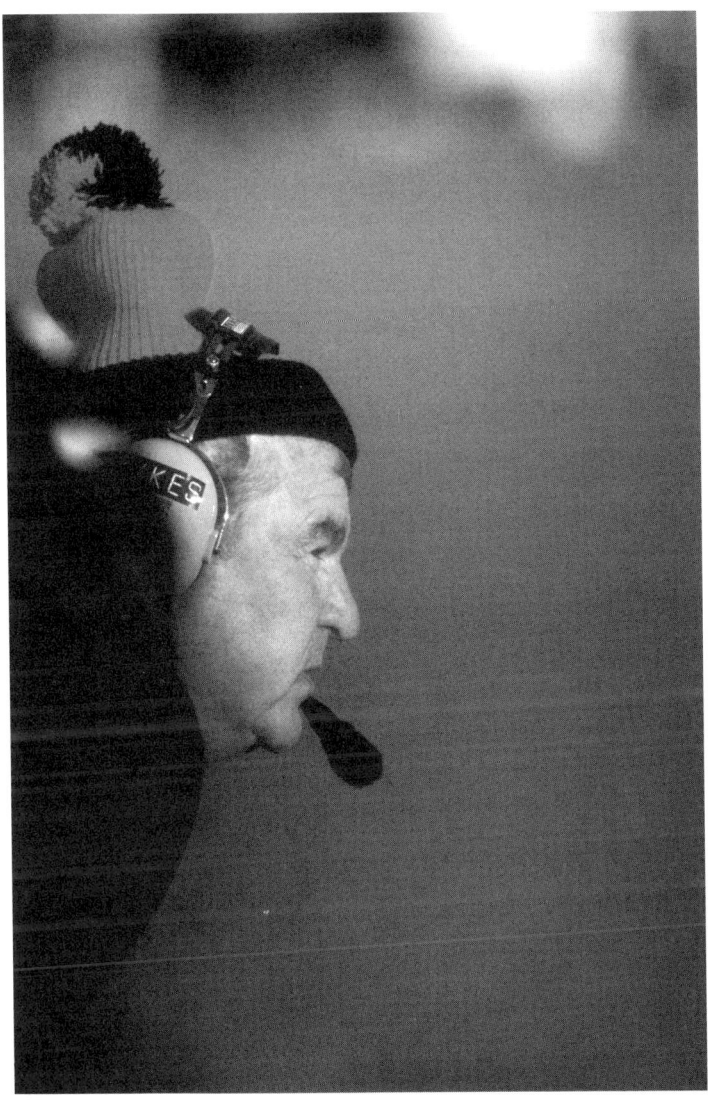

*Spike always knew what was going to happen with the weather.*
*(Stephen Dunn/Getty Images)*

*Texas Tech fans carrying the goal posts off the field. (AP/WWP)*

"Spike always had somebody on the staff call out to the Lubbock Airport before the game to get the latest report. Before the A&M game, he was told that the weather would change dramatically during the game, shifting to a 40 mile-per-hour gale.

"I think we beat the Aggies that day because we knew which way the wind was going to blow. Okay, maybe Sammy Morris's179 rushing yards had something to do with the 21-19 upset. But paying attention to details like the weather report was something that a lot of people didn't know about Spike."

## Tough Breaks

Sammy Morris was another one who showed his bravery and maturity in a different way. This kid repeatedly got a raw deal and did nothing but persevere through it without complaint.

He was a great football player, but when he came to Tech, he was told he needed to take a couple courses to be eligible. He did as he was told, but a counselor had made a mistake and he was actually ineligible.

Next year, it was the same thing. He did everything he was told to do, and still wasn't eligible. As it turned out, he used up three years of eligibility and never made it onto the field. In the first game his senior year, against Arizona State, he was injured before halftime and was out five or six games because of it.

He ended up helping us out quite a bit, though, as he pulled in a pass from Zebbie Lethridge for about 85 yards to beat Texas A&M in 1999.

The thing about Sammy Morris that was so impressive was the way he kept coming back. To lose your eligibility twice because of somebody else's mistake is an unbelievable chain of events. And I'll confess, there were times when it was hard for me to even look him in the face because of the bad deal he had gotten. Some kids would have sued the university or the NCAA. Some kids would have just quit.

But Sammy Morris, who was dealt a bad, bad, bad hand, kept his mouth shut and continued working. That's the kind of character and determination that landed him work in the National Football League.

# Swan Song Against the Sooners

It had gotten out a little bit that I was probably going to retire. But I didn't want to take anything away from the kids, so I didn't say anything about it until after the game. I felt sad, sure, because I had a lot of fun coaching.

What was so exciting was the way these kids responded to the challenge of the Oklahoma game.

# E.J. Speaks

I'm not so sure that the last game I coached, against Oklahoma in 1999, wasn't the best example of a second half turning a game around in our favor.

We were down 28-7 at half against an Oklahoma team that would go on to win a national championship the next season. We had a freshman quarterback in Kliff Kingsbury, so it was hard to imagine us mounting some huge rally.

But we somehow got an unexpected lift from a surprise speaker at halftime. E.J. Holub, who is probably the best player to ever play at Texas Tech and tougher than an acre of garlic, came up to me and said, "Coach, let me talk to these guys before they go out." And, man, did he unleash a speech.

He told them to get their rears in gear and go out and win this game. It was entirely impromptu and unrehearsed ... and he used some extremely strong words. We came out and something good happened early and we went on to beat them 38-28.

It was the best reversal of fortune I'd ever seen, and it's clear we've got E.J. Holub and his tough-love motivation to thank for it.

# Chapter 26

# Moving On

## Stepping Down

You can sense it; you can tell when it's time to go. Or at least you should be able to. Some coaches miss the timing, or they refuse to pay attention to it, and that can get to be an ugly situation.

I loved Texas Tech to the point that it had become a part of me. It was a dream to get the job, and I had an unbelievable time coaching there. The year I quit at Tech, one guy on our staff had been working with me since 1966, one since 1967, one since 1968, and another guy had been at Tech for 16 years. My son, Rick, was also on the staff. That's stability; that's a bunch of good people for whom loyalty and trust was never an issue. That's a rare thing in college football.

I was never one to worry much about my contract, but I'm glad I had one. Athletic director T Jones gave me a 10-year contract and that provided security. But while I was there, we went through four or five presidents and four ath-

*Spike spent 13 years as the head coach of Texas Tech. (Photo courtesy of Spike Dykes)*

letic directors. Now, you know that those people may have wanted somebody who was their own guy—not me—as their football coach. That's the way it is.

You always have some battles along the way, too. Money is a big deal in college athletics. I'd have to say our facilities were adequate (they're great now and getting better); our attendance was adequate; our record was adequate, but never as good as we would have liked.

I think I probably got a little stale, and when you do that, it's time to get somebody in there who is refreshed. You lose a few supporters every year, and I understand that. Good Lord, sometimes ugly is just ugly and you can't make ugly pretty if it ain't. We lost some games we should have won, too; nobody knew that more than I did.

I never had any pressure other than the sort of pressure that coaches all self-impose. But I would still imagine some of the folks in the administration were relieved when I left. It was time for a fresh start for Tech. The phrase they always use these days is: Take it to the next level. You know, we did a lot of great things in 13 years, and I know we elevated the program. But we weren't quite at that "next level," so why not see if somebody else can't do it?

I have to say it was mostly a mutual admiration society when I left, but I still imagine there were two or three people on that board of directors who were tickled to death that I decided to step down.

You know, really, what I think pushed me over the edge more than anything was that I never spent much time with my wife. Being gone all the time keeps you apart. I thought it was time to remedy that.

# My Time at Tech

Yes, I obviously had a special feeling about Texas Tech. I always felt that what makes colleges are the people. We had great people and great students. Texas Tech is a regional school and it's in an area where there aren't many other options.

It makes a really warm environment; it's a place that makes you feel at home. There is a warmth on the campus and a good feeling between the community and the school. The city was proud of the school, and the school served a valuable service for a lot of people.

There was a wholesome feeling to it, and I always felt it was a wonderful, wonderful school filled with good people. That's really what made it feel special.

# Fishin', Golfin', and Screwin' Around

To be honest, I never really cared for the idea of being one of those coaches who works the sidelines until he's worn down, finally retires, and then keels over the next week. There's too much golf and fishing to do for a man to go that route.

I started coaching in 1959 and coached through the 1999 season. That's 41 football seasons. That's plenty for anybody.

How do I fill my time now? By not worrying about filling my time. The big thing is that my calendar isn't packed with obligations. And I don't have to spend all those nights in motels on the road trying to woo some 17 year old. Coaching Texas Tech is a hard job in a lot of ways; you have got to be diligent on that road recruiting, and you have to make a lot of public appearances. Those rubber-chicken dinners alone can darn near kill a coach.

Coach Darrell Royal quit Texas when he was in his early 50s, and I was with him one time when somebody asked him if he regretted quitting too early. He said, "Nah, never, I did some things I wanted to do, and had a real plateful. Nah, it was time to go." I admired that.

Now, I don't do a darn thing, just play golf, go fishin' and screw around.

You know ... just living a little bit.


# The Fir Was Named Douglas


Yes, I was born in Lubbock and loved working there. So people ask me why I retired to Horseshoe Bay.

Well, it's about 40 miles west of Austin in the hill country. I had a friend who had a house down here years ago and I got familiar with it. There are three golf courses and there's a lake and a lot of amenities. It's pretty, too. There are a few things we have in Horseshoe Bay we didn't have in West Texas ... flowers, hills, deer and trees. As much as I loved Lubbock, there were only four trees in the whole town, and I knew 'em all by name.

# A Good Walk Enhanced

When you've been a competitive person all your life, it's hard to get old and do nothing but sit around and play bridge or something. When you get to my age, if you're not careful, there's not much you can do to be competitive. Golf supplies that for me.

I'm an 11 handicap, but it's mostly just for fun. There's so much of it that is about the flow of your mentality. One day you can't make a putt and two days later you can't miss one, but you hit four balls out of bounds off the tee. I think that's the greatest appeal … nobody can really master it. It's a great challenge and it's different every day.

Son Rick Dykes on Spike's approach to golf: *"If you've seen that scene in the movie* Tin Cup *where the guy keeps trying to hit the ball over the water … that's dad. If he's got 240 [yards] to go over the water, he'll go for it every time. I've seen him empty his bag of balls trying to make that shot. He'll stand there and hit it until he runs out of balls."*

# Travels with Spike

When a football schedule and recruiting and all that goes with the job of being a coach does not anchor you down, you can get out and try a few new things.

My wife and I, for instance, drive out in the country sometimes and look at wild flowers. How's that for a symbol of total tranquility? And the worst thing about it is that I entirely enjoyed it. It used to be the only flowers I noticed were the ones they used to dress up the lateral hazards on the side of fairways. But this was out in the country, and we go out there specifically to look at them. I'm surprised I'm willing to let anybody know about it … I guess that's a sign you really are getting old and beat up and worn out.

Now, I always thought I'd rather go to El Paso than Europe, but we went over there and when we saw Normandy, it changed my entire perspective on what life is all about. I'm a flag-waving American, and I'll tell you, being there at Omaha Beach humbled me like few other things. It was one of the most moving days of my life.

Three days later we went down to that place where Monet painted all those flowers, in what was supposed to be the most beautiful gardens in the world. Know what? We've got prettier flowers right here in Horseshoe Bay. That's what I think, at least.

Former athletic director T Jones on Spike's legacy at Tech: *"What he left them with was a winning attitude. He had a very positive and upbeat approach. He had a wonderful staff, too. He was so close to them, and not just the coaches, but also the families, the wives and the kids. He tried everything he could to help them with their salaries. With his portion of the money from football camps, he would spread it around to his assistants. That was his money and he could do with it as he pleased, and he wanted to help them. I know they appreciated it."*

Former quarterback Billy Joe Tolliver on Spike's lasting influence: *"Spike Dykes helped me by being a great salesman. I bought everything he was selling. He said a lot of things that made a helluva lot of sense. I remember the lectures he would give to the team and to this day I catch myself using some of them on my own kids. The one that sticks out the most is about doing the right thing.*

*"He used to say, 'Fellas, do you think it's easy to be a drug addict or an alcoholic? MY LANDS, NO! It can't be easy trying to figure out how you're gonna get your next high. It can't be easy feeling the way a junkie feels most of the time. It ain't easy to be always plottin' and schemin' the whole time you know deep down that you ain't doin' right. Well, let me tell you, it ain't easy doing the right thing, either. It's hard to walk the straight and narrow. It's difficult to be a stand-up guy, a man. So if that's the case, it seems to me that we all should try that right way. If they are both hard, why wouldn't you do the one that keeps your ox out of a ditch?' That has always stuck with me. It isn't hard to do the right. It is hard to know what's right. But once you know what's right, it is hard NOT to do it."*

## What It Meant

If I look back at my career at Tech, the thing that nobody will ever be able to know is what we did to get ourselves into the Big 12 Conference. We started playing good non-conference teams, and that brought us some respectability that was crucial. We started getting the attendance up and getting more competitive. I don't think they would have had us in the Big 12 if we hadn't followed that path.

Only twice in all those years did we finish in the bottom half of our division, no matter which conference we were in, and that was important. And that was something that could be a little hard to do at Tech.

We dang sure competed well against our rivals, going nearly .500 against Texas and Texas A&M. In fact, we beat the Aggies four of the last five times we played them. I know that was something new for Red Raider fans.

Any degree of success we had was attributable to the hard work of my coaching staff; they were good people who loved football and loved coaching kids.

I guess if there was anything remarkable about my years at Texas Tech it was the fact that I survived through four university presidents and four athletic directors. I guess there was enough turnover there that they didn't have enough time to get tired of me.

It allowed me to always stay at least a couple steps ahead of the posse … and loving it every step of the way.

# Spike-ism

I won a spelling bee one time. I was in first grade. Of course, there were only two of us in the class. But I won.

# Celebrate the Heroes of Texas Sports
## in These Other Releases from Sports Publishing!

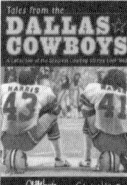